We're On Our Way USA

Andy C Wareing

Copyright

Andy C Wareing

Cover design by Andy C Wareing

Contents

To our friend, Coach Dave McAuley

1937 – 2019

"Low to your toe, High to the sky"

A Rubicon

My head ached and the sore hands that held the glass were heavily bandaged. It began, as many things, both good and occasionally bad do, with one glass of red wine and a gin and tonic too many, shared over a late chippy tea in our little Victorian brick semi-detached house. Our two boys were both upstairs, asleep in bed, and we were trying to relax after another long week. The last 48 hours had not gone well. For me, a Rubicon had been crossed, a tipping point reached, and we were busy making a new plan for a different life.

The English house we were seated in that night was the second one we had bought together. It was located on busy Sussex Road in the town of Southport, in the drippy grey northwest of England. It was the town we had been born in, grown up in, got married in, and in which we had bought our first house together. It was the town of our parents and our grandparents and who knew how many generations before. I was always tempted to research my family tree, thinking we might be descended from Norse warriors or Norman princes, but initial searches showed not the slightest trace of blue blood, only that my predecessors were more likely to have helped populate the Australian penal colonies of the late 18th century.

The night before, I had returned home from the most fruitless and yet bone-fatiguing meeting I had ever had the misfortune to almost attend. The day had begun at five in the morning when I had jumped in my company car and driven twenty frosty and winter-darkened miles to Wigan train station. I waited on a darkened station platform that had been tastefully decorated with discarded crisp bags and dog ends, with a miserable, silent huddle of like-minded commuters, zombified by the combination of the weather and the hour, waiting for the train that was already predictably late.

The Virgin diesel train eventually arrived and we all boarded in an angry, fuming silence to take defensive positions on seats, with briefcases and travel bags used as fortifications and barricades so that nobody else could, God forbid, have the temerity to seek comfort on the seats next to us.

The service had trundled its way through the Midlands, in the unconcerned about the timetable manner that only British trains can, occasionally stopping in between stations for no reason of sufficient importance that would prompt the guard to announce an explanation. We eventually arrived, four hours later and an entire forty-five minutes late at Euston train station in London.

The station concourse of Euston was then, and always will be, a vast melee, a sweating, surging, hurrying cross-section of the British population. Tramps and the homeless milled about amongst the business-people and the tourists. Everybody is always in everybody else's way, like a human murmuration but without the instinct and coordination that gives the starlings their wonder.

I elbowed my way to the entrance to the tube station and navigated the steep and seemingly interminable escalators and creepy Victorian tunnels, white tiled, decorated and smelling like the inside of a gent's toilet, to eventually shoulder my way onto an over-crowded and noisy tube train. With standing room only, I swayed, pressed together like deodorized tinned ham against my other passengers on the Northern Line.

We jiggled our slow way beneath the streets of the capital for fifteen minutes to reach Embankment and then I scampered through more subterranean tunnels, for all the world like a giant lab rat seeking its cheese treat, to take a District Line train west. Through more tunnels and then occasionally rising up to pass through rows of dilapidated smoke-stained brick houses and industrial units, we roughly followed the meander of the Thames, all the way to the still crowded and urban periphery of the city.

The customer I was visiting was Centrica who own British Gas amongst others, and it had been made clear to me that my presence at the meeting was critical to its successful goal of selling them more of our dodgy software.

The District Line train took forty minutes more and then I accidentally got off the train, one station too early. I realized I was horribly late for the meeting, so began jogging the mile or so to their offices located just off the high street. It took me another frenzied, watch checking fifteen minutes, mopping the sweat from my brow and trying frantically to dry the damp patches beneath my arms, to clear security.

Seven solid hours of stress-filled travel later I opened the door to the meeting room and, I shit you not, as I did so, all of the participants stood, closed laptops and notebooks and shook hands. I had missed the whole bloody thing. Apparently, they had somehow managed just fine without me.

It was after seven in the evening, fourteen hours later, that I pulled my Audi back into the drive, turned off the ignition and sat there in the dark, banging my head slowly and without rhythm onto the steering wheel, while my wife, Paula, stood at the living room window, knowing I had gone insane, but wondering what had finally pushed me over the edge.

The next day I had another meeting with Centrica, but this time in Sheffield. It had snowed overnight so I slid my way across the hills of the Pennines in my faithful Audi. I parked up at a Little Chef to meet the salesperson, a guy called Julian and a couple from Cable & Wireless who were our partners in the deal.

For those readers not familiar with the concept of a Little Chef, it is similar in concept to an American Waffle House, but the waitresses generally carry less firearms and the floors have 100% less waffle batter spilled on them. Little Chefs used to be dotted around the highways and byways of England, selling overpriced eggs and bacon to weary travelers. Those of us who frequented them often, jokingly referred to them as 'Little Thieves.'

Me and Julian met Ian and Julie over the 'Olympic Breakfast' option and we briefed the meeting that would soon take place in the city fifteen miles away. Parking was at a premium in Sheffield so I left my Audi in the parking lot and jumped in Julian's BMW. Ian and Julie jumped in Ian's Range Rover Freelander and they led us out of the car park towards the slip road that would take us down onto the busy dual carriageway.

Snow was still falling, a light dusting that refused, for the better part, to stick. It created a greasy grey slush that stained the sides of the wet roads. Julian pulled onto the slip road and gunned the BMW to catch up with Ian. The BMW understeered in the slippery conditions and then, when Julian over corrected, it immediately oversteered and we crashed heavily into a concrete bollard that supported the Armco barrier. The force of the collision flipped the BMW onto its roof and suddenly I found myself sliding, inverted, down the sloping slip road, hanging suspended from my seat belt, using both my hands to protect my bald head from the remarkable amount of windscreen glass that Julian had created when he smashed it with his forehead, having failed to fasten his seatbelt when he set off.

We slid for thirty feet down the slip road. Wind and sleet blew through the smashed windscreen, mobile phones and loose coins rained down from upturned pockets. I was stunned and disoriented, time seemed to slow, a stop frame animation, the grating noise of the roof on the graveled tarmac deafening and pervasive. We finally came to a hushed stop and I hung against gravity, bewildered, from my seat belt smelling for the faintest tinge of spilt gas that might hint at fire.

After a few minutes, Ian appeared at my window and pulled the door open. He reached inside to release my seatbelt and I slumped to the roof in an untidy heap of bleeding and bruised limbs. Already I could hear the sirens of the ambulance and with Ian's help I crawled out to sit in a numb silence on the muddy bank by the side of the road, shivering in my suit jacket as the sleet fell, thick and frigid around me.

Inside the ambulance, I was fully conscious and aware so I was left alone for the initial part of the journey. Julian had been rendered unconscious when his head had smashed the windscreen and the paramedics were busy with him for the first ten minutes of the ride to the hospital. Finally, with Julian stabilized, the paramedic took a moment to check my wounds. The backs of my hands and fingers were badly lacerated from where I had coddled and protected my head from the glass and I had a couple of puncture wounds to my scalp but I felt fine. The paramedic shone a light in both eyes to check if I was in shock or suffering from a concussion, which I was not.

I had lost most of my hair in my twenties, but thought I had a nicely shaped head, at least until the paramedic asked me, with a curious and concerned look in her eyes, thinking perhaps that I had fractured my skull in several places, "has your head always been that shape?"

Sheffield A&E patched me up, and that same night I released myself in order to drive home, on the promise that I would turn myself into a local hospital closer to home the following day to have ligaments checked and hands and fingers stitched. Ian dropped me at my car and was good enough to follow me most of the way home, back across the now darkened M62, just in case delayed shock rendered me suddenly doolally, and I drove myself off the motorway and into a ditch.

I had called Paula from the hospital to warn her of the crash and my condition, and as I pulled the Audi back up our driveway, she and the kids were waiting for me even though it was very late. I was fine. Just bruised, bloodied and bandaged, sore and pissed off. She had the chippy tea ready and a bottle of red wine open.

It was that same night that we decided to emigrate. To sell up and ship out. We had talked about doing it several times before, usually late at night after a few drinks. Canada perhaps, maybe even Spain, or New Zealand or Australia, anything was possible. But the next day life generally got in the way of pursuing any alcohol-fueled plans and it was all forgotten in the hubbub of busy lives. But not this night. This night was different.

During our discussion the one country we had initially ruled out as an option was the United States of America. For no good reason other than our view, as foreigners, was colored by the TV shows and the news—too much gun violence, too oddly religious, a wealthy nation, blessed by its own relentless self-belief and undying optimism for sure, but also one that had such bizarre politics that its elections appeared to us, when viewed through the lens of the media, like one vast game show, one where even the starring lead actor from 'Bedtime for Bonzo' could become leader of the free world.

Regardless, after the last few days, it was an exciting and ridiculously compelling idea and we chatted about the possibilities late into the night. We just needed to figure out how to make such a thing happen.

A Passing

The year we finally decided to 'just go for it' was 2006. That year had been as awful as life can sometimes be. After an initial but debilitating stroke my dad had been hospitalized with heart failure. He had lingered, never giving up the hope that he would be allowed to return to the home he had long shared with my Mum, who had died ten years before him, which, of course, he sadly never did. Towards the end, his faltering heart and plummeting blood pressure caused vivid hallucinations, but he was spared from seeing anything scary, he just saw, and heard bluebirds. They flew around the shared ward in the hospital. They perched on the end of his bed and trilled and sang to him.

"Somebody must have left a window open again."

"Yeah, that's right Dad."

"They sing lovely though, don't they?"

"They do Dad. They do."

"When will they let me go home."

"I don't know Dad; I'll ask a nurse for you when we leave tonight."

Heartbreaking.

His heart finally betrayed all of his hopes of returning home and broke for good on a beautiful spring day. Paula called me as soon as she heard the news from the hospital. I was three-hundred miles away, again driving my Audi to yet another bullshit meeting. Given the constraints of the British Isles, I was as far from Dad as it was possible to be. I turned around as fast as I could and broke every speed limit to get back to the hospital but I knew, deep down, that I was already far too late.

The only light side was at the funeral. I had ordered flowers to spell out 'GRANDAD' to be displayed on the side of the hearse, a parting gift and gesture from our two boys, his grandchildren, Ben and Adam. Unfortunately, without telling us, when the flowers were delivered to the funeral directors, they found that they didn't quite fit on the car and had decided that the best course of action was to split them in two. You could see folks by the side of the road scratching their heads and wondering what terrible, single tragedy had visited itself upon this poor family, as a hearse carrying only a single coffin rolled by, with one side of the hearse spelling out 'GRAN' and the other side spelling out 'DAD'. Sometimes you just can't make shit like that up.

And then Paula's mum died, followed shortly after by her dear old dad. In the span of a few short months, together we had organized and wept through three funerals, three wakes, one court inquest, applied for probate, emptied the contents of two houses, sold those two houses, sold two cars, and distributed the remaining assets of wills and personal mementos to our other siblings.

If there ever is the slightest of a plus side to such things, with no surviving parents we no longer had ties that bound us in the awkward tangles of responsibility. I had one brother and Paula had three sisters but they all had lives and children of their own. I was 40 years old at the time, the moment to try something different was upon us.

I made an appointment to see my manager, and the next time I was in the Leatherhead office I sat down with him and talked it through. I was somewhat lucky in that my manager at the time had been given the same opportunity at a different company, to the one I was pursuing. Steve had lived and worked in Chicago for a few years.

"I want to see if the company would be supportive of a secondment, a chance for me to gain some international experience."

"OK, I guess, at least in theory that's possible. Where are you thinking?"

"Canada would be ideal."

"We don't really have an office in Canada, that territory is managed out of the United States."

"Spain?"

"No chance."

"Australia or New Zealand?"

"They just made a bunch of people redundant."

"Then where would you suggest?"

"We might be able to find a position for you in Japan."

"Japan? I think that might be too much of a cultural leap for the kids."

What we had neglected to get right for an international move was the age of our two boys. Ben was already fourteen and Adam was eleven at the time. They were both in high school and a move to another country would be far from seamless for them. They had a ton of friends and were well-settled into the schools and lives they had created for themselves.

"If Japan is no good, the best option we might be able to offer would be a transfer to the USA."

Of course. The one country we had already ruled out as an option. "Let me think about it."

On my way out of the office, I bumped into our then CEO, a huge guy called Nick. He was large in both frame, character and voice. He was a few years younger than me but through being a ruthless, bloody-minded force of nature he had risen to run the entire company. Nobody could decide if he wore a wig or not, but given his personal wealth, if his hair was real, it was quite the statement piece. It sat like a small, shaggy and furious Scottish Terrier on the very crown of his scalp and appeared to remain still no matter in which direction Nick turned his head. He could be an absolute nightmare to work for and could often be heard shouting at one of the salespeople for missing a sales target. Grown men were often seen coming out of his office in tears never to be seen or heard from again. You crossed Nick precisely one time only. So far, I had avoided doing so and we had a good relationship. He trusted me and I trusted him.

"Wareing!" he boomed.

"Hi Nick."

"What are you here for? Centrica meeting?"

"Actually, I was just talking to Steve about a potential move. To go work for the company in a different territory, maybe get some international experience."

"Well, be sorry to see you go of course," he went quiet for a moment, "America for you I think." And with that he was gone, storming off down the corridor to flay the skin from another poor performing salesperson. I sensed that a decision, like it or not, had just been made for me.

Back home Paula and I talked about it at length as we sat on the sofa cuddling our two pups, our lovely Cavalier King Charles Spaniels, Bandit and Scout, while at the same time being largely ignored by our ginger cat, the ones the kids had named Tiny Winky. Maybe the USA wouldn't be as bad as it was portrayed on Miami Vice, Hill Street Blues, Dexter and Breaking Bad. And we did know *one* American. One of my previous bosses had been one after all, a big black gay guy called Kevin and we liked *him* enough.

We decided to test the water. I had been to the States a few times for work and Paula had been for a day or two here and there, but we had never been together as a couple on a vacation. The corporate office was in Roswell. Not the Roswell located in New Mexico, where all the top-secret flying saucers are stored in Area 51 by those conniving fiends in the Federal Government, but the other one, the one secreted amongst the trees in the peach state of Georgia, about twenty miles north of the city of Atlanta.

And so too was Kevin, our one American friend, so we decided to spend a few days there, check out some of the sub-divisions, get a handle on property layouts and prices. I might even try to set up a couple of informal interviews with some folks I knew at the office. It would be a chance to see if anybody had any open headcount and would be willing for me to fill one of them for a year or two.

An American Vacation

The Boeing 737 touched down with a bump and a shriek of tires in Hartsfield Jackson airport in the early afternoon and, after slowly clearing customs, we walked together out of the chill of the air conditioning and into the unfamiliar, all enveloping embrace of the furnace blast of the day. There was a stiff wind from the south and the sensation was like being trapped inside a giant hairdryer.

We picked up the convertible Sebring I had reserved at the rental car lot and, after climbing in the right-hand side of the car and finding no steering wheel there, I got back out and tried the left-hand side. We navigated out of the crowded loops of the airport and we joined the press of traffic on I-85 north.

I had often driven in Europe, even in such manic cities as Rome and Paris, but this was my first time driving in the United States and, if I am honest, Atlanta in rush hour was a bit of a surprise to both the senses and the sphincter. I-85 was packed (I found out much later that it always is), six lanes of traffic in both directions, all intent on passing each other simultaneously. Traffic overtook and undertook, cars swerved across four lanes indicating right but heading left. Some cars seemed to have just left the indictors on, permanently blinking the potential for a future change of lane for all eternity. Semis, forty feet long pushed aggressively into spaces thirty feet too short. Young black guys driving repurposed ex-police Crown Victoria's had seats so far reclined only the tops of their heads and their fingers on the tops of steering wheels were visible.

Nobody seemed to be paying the slightest bit of attention to the road. We saw car after car, hurtling down the outside lane, suddenly seeming to realize that their exit junction was about to be missed; they would swerve across all five lanes, testing the reflexes and loudness of the horns of all the other road users. Everybody, *everybody*, held a mobile phone clamped to an ear and sipped on a steaming cup of Starbucks.

We drove past Turner Field, the baseball stadium, and passed the golden dome of city hall. The sun was still high in a brilliant clear sky. The skyscrapers of downtown gradually gave way to the office buildings and condominiums of midtown. The traffic was either a mass of fast-moving mayhem or completely stationary.

I tried to play it cool. This was, after all, the country and probably the city I was asking Paula to make her home, and driving here was a requirement. But by the time we made it all the way through the city and pulled off our junction onto Haynes Bridge Road, and into the car park of the Embassy Suites Hotel, my shirt was drenched, my head throbbed and my whitened knuckles ached.

We changed and showered and, yawning against the jet lag, we made our way to meet Kevin for a drink in the Rays Killer Creek restaurant on Mansell Road. It was a Friday night and the place was loud with the sound of folks happy to be out of the office, enjoying a cocktail before heading home for the weekend. We had a cocktail ourselves and then jumped in Kevin's Land Rover Discovery for a tour around the area.

"Here's your Kroger. This is where you will do all of your grocery shopping."

We took a walk inside and marveled at the pure amount of produce on display. The artificial thunder that boomed around the vegetable displays before the 'rainwater' freshened them with a good soaking; the forty different flavors of Kap'n Crunch; the truly insane number of varieties of Peanut Butter. In addition to the crunchy and smooth varieties we were familiar with in the UK there were Marmite flavored, Maple, Honey, Chipotle Honey, Pumpkin Pie Spice, Cinnamon crunch, Honey crunch, Oatmeal cookie, Rainbow cookie, Cookies & Cream, Birthday cake, Chocolate fudge, Chocolate maple pretzel, Mocha cappuccino, salted caramel, Cookie butter and something called S'mores.

Back on the road, Kevin kept up the tour.

"This is your Auto Zone; they have everything you need for your car."

"This is your CVS; this is where you can buy all of your medical supplies."

"Over there is your liquor store, that's where you will buy your...liquor."

"That over there is your Walmart. That's where you will buy...well, absolutely anything you want really."

We ended the tour at a vast car lot. I don't recall which one, but it was on the Alpharetta Highway where all of the car dealers in Roswell are clustered around the occasional Taqueria and Brazilian Wax outlet. To our pure English surprise, even though the dealership was closed, all of the cars were unlocked. A shocking idea in Britain, when even during office hours the keys to each locked car need to be requested from the oily sales team.

We spent a lovely hour, still bathed in the nighttime heat, listening to the cicadas. We sat in a Dodge Viper and a huge Hummer, the civilian and road legal version of the military Humvee. I stood by the grill of a bright blue Dodge RAM 1500 twin cab pickup truck and laughed at how big it was. The hood came up to the level of my neck and we joked about America and its obsession for all things enormous. I would never be seen dead driving something so big and obscene.

We were starving, so with the jet lag finally overcoming us, Kevin dropped us off at a Taco Mac restaurant close to the hotel and promised to meet us for a couple of drinks and dinner the following evening.

Inside was a typical American sports bar, all big screen TVs, a long bar and comfortable booths. Our chirpy waitress came over and after handing us menus and fetching a couple of beers for us, asked us what we wanted to eat.

"I'll have the wings please."

"Original, roasted or boneless?"

"Err, original?"

"All flats, all drums or a combo?"

She was fast losing me. I had no idea what she was talking about at this point. I didn't want a flat or a drum, I wanted chicken wings, "err, a combo please?"

"What sauce do you want hun?"

"Sauces? Well, what sauces are available?"

She rolled her eyes a little at this and pointed to the long list of sauce flavors, all with varying spice levels listed on the menus.

"Oh, jeez. One second." I scanned the menu hoping for inspiration. There was Mild Buffalo, Medium Buffalo and Hot Buffalo, Parmesan

Garlic, Asian Sweet Heat, Sweet Chili Sesame, BBQ, Honey Twang, Honey Chipotle, Habanero, Three-mile Island, Death Sauce, Slow Burn, Original Lemon Pepper, Chili Mango and Korean Black Garlic.

I knew that in my fatigued state that I didn't want Death Sauce and I didn't even know what buffalo tasted like. I had hoped for a quick bite to eat, not the Spanish Inquisition, because nobody ever expects that.

I sighed heavily, "Medium Buffalo please." In for a penny as they say. Buffalo flavored chicken, how uniquely and charmingly American.

"And what side?"

This was fast becoming tedious, but at least here I thought I was on safer ground, "fries please." I asked definitively.

"Sweet potato, tots, or regular?"

Another sigh from me, "regular."

"And that comes with either Ranch or Blue Cheese and either celery or carrot?"

And so, on it went. In America you get choice. A lot of it. In England you get to select a menu item as it is written on the menu and be bloody thankful for it. You can ask for something to be replaced or substituted, but your request will most often be met with a blank stare from the jaded and pimply creature who has been assigned to pretend to serve your table.

This plethora of choices was at first, tired as were, a chore to us, but I have to admit that when the food arrived it was delicious. It turned out that the peppery hot buffalo sauce was not made *from* buffalos but rather named for the city in New York State where it was invented. And the ranch? Dear God, I couldn't drench my fries in it and push them into my mouth quickly enough.

The waitress brought our check and we saw that she had signed it and written 'thanks' with a hand-drawn smiley face underneath. We were charmed and overtipped massively.

And then, with dinner done, we staggered back to our hotel and, with socks still on, we fell into our comfy bed and slipped into a deep and dreamless sleep.

An Exploration

We woke and had a leisurely coffee in the room. Through the tenth-floor bedroom windows, I looked out at an America waking and beginning a new day. The sun was already high and the buildings and roads gleamed with a blindingly reflected light. Old Glory was visible from at least twenty office buildings, fluttering in the warm breeze while black vultures soared on thermals in the perfectly clear cerulean sky. Everywhere was clean and bright. Compared to the grimy, drizzle-filled Victorian streets we had grown up in, the sight dazzled with hope and affluence.

It was exciting to think that we might live here, but at the same time, this close to North Point Mall as we were, this part of Roswell was dominated by highways, high rise and traffic and bustle. Our plan for the day was to pick under the scab, the surface veneer of ugly highway billboards and endless fast-food outlets that disguised the true America. To find the one where Americans really lived, hidden from those just passing through. We wanted to expose suburban America, for good or ill, to find the one where we might seek to make a home.

The day didn't start so auspiciously as I had inadvertently left on the lights of the Sebring and the car battery was flat. The rental company was useless but one of the friendly hotel workers was sent out with a set of jump leads, and after backing up his truck to park alongside he drawled, "lem-me give y'all nice folks a start and git y'all on your way."

It was a glorious day so we thought zooming around north Atlanta in the convertible might be the best thing ever. In the end it took us twenty minutes to get the top down. We wrestled with it, pushed and pulled handles, swung all my weight off the hinges but it just wouldn't budge. Then we saw the button on the dash. One press and the motor buzzed into life and the canvas top collapsed and folded itself elegantly into the boot. I put on my Ray-Bans and off we went to explore. Our first stop was at Wills Park Equestrian Center.

Fifteen minutes later in the gargantuan and entirely empty parking lot of Wills Park, we put the top back up. The sun, even at ten in the morning, was ferocious in a way I had never experienced, and despite being bathed in factor 1000, my bald head was already steaming and suppurating like molten lava across my tortured scalp.

Paula had found the equestrian center on Google and, being a keen horse rider in the UK, wanted to check out what an American riding school might look like. There was no sign of life as we got out of the car but we walked across to the rows of stables undaunted. The place was huge. Row upon row of well-maintained stalls, two practice menages, and one truly enormous, floodlit, and fully covered menage. But not a single horse to be seen. There was nobody there and no sign that any horses had used the facility in months. No sounds or smells of horses, no piles of horse crap, no grooms. We stood in the sunshine scratching our heads. In the UK it would be insanity to have such a wonderfully provisioned and spacious facility just sat unused, but that certainly seemed to be the case here.

Confused, we spent the morning driving around in aimless circles, turning off to explore random neighborhoods. They were all neat and tidy with perfectly manicured lawns. All filled with detached houses and all, at least to UK standards, absolutely massive. But the same feeling of abandonment and emptiness. No people walking dogs, or just simply walking. Nobody doing yard work, nobody washing cars. All morning we looked at beautiful sub-divisions and houses we could only dream of owning in the UK, wondering if perhaps, overnight, aliens had abducted the entire population.

We saw a sign for Roswell Park, and on a whim turned in and parked up by the tennis center. We walked around, marveling at the twelve courts, the stadium seating, the floodlights and neat fencing. Everything here was immaculate, freshly painted, and diligently maintained. In the stifling heat, we walked the gravel path that led around the park. Two football fields, a lacrosse field, three baseball fields, an outdoor Olympic swimming pool, and a pretty fountain, dead center in the middle of a flat lake, that threw chuckling water high into the shimmering summer air, all set beneath the backdrop of yet another fluttering, gigantic American flag.

All of this infrastructure in a public park and just us two to marvel at it all. Not a single soul to be seen.

In the UK, the best a public park could offer would have been a single, moss-covered tennis court that hadn't sported a net for twelve years, a muddy footy pitch covered in weeds, beer cans, and dog shit, and a set of rusty children's swings and a dilapidated seesaw. But there would've been people there. The swings would have been taken over by a gang of feral twelve-year old's threatening to lighten your pockets at knifepoint if you got too close, and the park's only other occupants would have been a bunch of bored teenage mums, smoking and gossiping while pushing snotty babies around in prams, but my point is still valid. In an English park, even allowing for the limits on enjoyment it imposed, there would have been people. Every place we explored here was impressive, but where were all the folks to enjoy it?

We stumbled upon a Wendy's burger joint which was great, although for the life of us, we couldn't understand why the patty was square but the bun circular. We filled two cups the size of dustbins with Coca-Cola, the only fizzy beverage available anywhere in Atlanta. You wont find a Pepsi product anywhere within 100 miles of Atlanta, it being the international headquarters for Coca-Cola. When our cups were empty and we were ready to leave, we stood, feeling like criminals to fill them back up again, glancing nervously at the spotty youth at the checkout counter, waiting for him to scold us or ask us to pay. Of course, he didn't, not in the land of endless free refills and 'to-go' cups.

Re-fueled, and with a straining bladder, we continued our little tour of the subdivisions and shopping outlets around Roswell, Crabapple and Alpharetta. We had no idea where we were or where we were going, and we must have crisscrossed our own path continuously until, exhausted, we ended up back at the hotel.

We had some research to do before we were scheduled to meet Kevin for dinner. He had offered us the services of a realtor he had used before. Her name was Wendi and she had kindly offered to show us around some houses, the following day if we could pick four or five off the internet and send her the listing details. We duly did so, all properties based around the Roswell area, all detached, but a mix of big and small, ranch and traditional.

We showered and changed and then went downstairs into the lobby to wait for Kevin to pick us up. In the lobby, the hotel was just opening up for the resident's happy hour. When we arrived at ten to six it was deserted, but by the time the bar opened, the hotel's rooms had emptied, and a crowd of what seemed to be mostly British people had crowded there to enjoy the free drinks. At seven, when the free drinks stopped, the bar emptied as quickly as it had filled. Three or four drinks in, we heard Kevin beeping his horn and we turned to see his Discovery parked up outside.

Dinner was enjoyed seated outside a Taqueria. We ate fajitas and dipped salty tortilla chips into freshly made guacamole as the sun set the sky ablaze. I drank ice-cold beers and Kevin and Paula sipped frozen margaritas big enough to drown in, as the light failed and the restaurant's twinkling lights sprang into life. Kevin thought the restaurant might be short-changing the amount of tequila in the margaritas so he ordered extra shots and stirred them into the mix. We ordered more guac and more margaritas as the concrete slowly released the heat of the day. We chatted and laughed and mopped sweat from our brows and finally, with the restaurant staff stacking long vacated chairs and brushing the patio at our feet we took the hint and staggered home.

A False Start

All things considered; we woke up feeling not too bad. And we were excited. This morning Wendi was picking us up and we were going house hunting. In America! We made coffee and showered and were waiting in the lobby when Wendi's silver Jaguar XJ8 rolled up. We said our hellos and our introductions and Wendi handed us a bunch of printouts showing the listing details of the houses we had picked out the evening before. She was sweet, around our age, and as Georgian as can be.

Paula and I jumped in the back of the Jag and off we went in the direction of Roswell to see the first house. The day was already hot and the inside of the car was heating up too. I asked Wendi to turn up the A/C but the back of the car continued to swelter. The big Jag had soft suspension and we bounced lazily over every bump and ripple in the tarmac. Wendi kept up a continuous line of chatty questioning. Did we have kids? What age were they? Did I need ready access to the airport if we did move across?

Paula had fallen strangely silent and I was left to answer most of Wendi's questions. When I looked across, I realized why she was so quiet. Paula had turned a shade of virulent green that a paint manufacturer might creatively call *Kermit*. She had her handbag open and was preparing herself to fill it with last night's guacamole.

Luckily, at that very moment, with a lurch and a bump, Wendi pulled the big Jag into the drive of the first house on our list. It was a big two-storey house, brick fronted with siding. Two windows on either side of the brightly painted blue front door and two more upstairs.

Wendi pulled open the screen door and fiddled with the realtor lock to find and remove the front door key and twenty seconds later we were inside. After some time, we came to call this layout typical American because, at least in Georgia, many houses followed the exact same layout. Front door leading to an entryway with stairs to the second floor directly in front. Room off to the right, usually a dining room, and a room off to the left, this one almost never used and usually dressed as a snug or an office. In the back would be a kitchen and a great room, usually with a floor-to-ceiling, sometimes double-height picture window. Over time we may have come to think of that layout as typically American, but on that very first viewing of our very first American house, it took our breath away. It was enormous.

Unfortunately, Paula's queasy condition had not abated. We had only just got through the front door and Paula was already asking Wendi where the bathroom was. Wendi had missed the clues in the car that hinted at Paula's intense nausea, brought on by the false start hangover, and jollied into motion by the bumpy Jag. Wendi smiled and pointed at a door by the side of the entrance to the kitchen.

"Oh, right there, honey."

Paula almost pushed Wendi out of the way in her rush to get to the toilet and slammed and locked the door behind her. Wendi looked at me quizzically and then realized what was happening as we both studiously pretended not to hear the sounds of distress coming from the bathroom.

"BLOOOOOAAARGH —Flush."

"My, these ceilings look freshly painted, don't they?"

"They do, and I love the crown moldings."

"HUUUURRRPP. COUGH — Flush."

"Are these hardwood floors or laminates?"

"Oh, those are all hardwoods. Oak, I think, Pretty, aren't they?"

"GAAAACK. GAACK. BLAAARGH — Flush."

"They are very pretty. Can I take a look at the kitchen?"

This went on for a while, me making hopeless small talk with this woman I had known for all of fifteen minutes, while Paula tested to the limits the capacity and flushing efficiency of American sanitary ware and its associated plumbing.

Luckily for us, Wendi was a hardened campaigner of drinking frozen margaritas with Kevin, so was very understanding when Paula did finally come out of the bathroom dabbing the corner of her mouth with a piece of snow-white toilet paper, the same color as her cheeks.

"Sorry," Paula mumbled.

"Well, just bless your heart sweety, that's OK. Come on, let's take a look at this house together."

We walked around the house in awe. Every room was vast with high ceilings. The five bedrooms were spacious, a couple fitted with beautiful En-suites. The house had a double garage and workshop with electric doors. All sat on nearly half an acre. Back in England, this house would have been an entirely unaffordable million-pound dream for us.

We thought we had seen everything and nodded our satisfaction to Wendi who pointed to a door we had missed.

"Don't you wanna see the basement?"

I opened the door to find a set of stairs that led downwards into the basement. At the bottom, I found a gargantuan open space used as a gymnasium and next door to that a cinema room with a projector and reclining seats. Next to that was a small kitchen and bathroom with a shower. At the back of the house, double doors led out to the landscaped garden. I shouted up to Paula.

"There's an entire other house down here."

An Interview

In the end, we viewed all five houses and it soon became apparent that for the two or three years of my contract abroad, we could live like kings. If that was, I could secure a similar salary, or better, to what I was earning in the United Kingdom. Now I just needed to see if I could find a job that would provide that to me.

The next day I dropped Paula off at the Bahama Breeze restaurant across the street from the hotel and drove to the office, located at that time on Mansell Road. I had two meetings arranged and was hopeful that either one or the other would result in a position being offered.

The first meeting I had scheduled was with an old friend called John who used to work in the UK and had emigrated a few years back. I met him in his office and we chatted for a while about things back home and who was doing what to who, and who had got themselves sacked because of it. The usual stuff. And then it got a little awkward as I tried to pin John down on whether he might have an open position, and if he did, would I stand a chance at securing it. John hummed and hawed for a while and made noises that he was certain, absolutely positive, that if I moved across to the USA, I would then be able to get a job, somewhere, just fine.

Of course, that's *not* how it works in America. Unless you are willing to swim the Rio Grande under the cover of darkness, to live and work in America you *need* a Visa.

There are many, many visas available to those wishing to move to, and work or study, in the United States, but they all fall into two broad categories, Non-Immigrant Visas and Immigrant Visas.

The main difference is that on an immigrant visa, entry to the USA automatically grants the holder the right to apply for a Permanent Resident Card (PRC), more commonly known as the famous green Card. And that can be a very big advantage. If you have the choice, go for an immigrant visa.

On the other hand, if you enter on a non-immigrant visa, you are by definition, only going to be in the USA on a temporary basis.

Immigrant visas include the K-1 visa, also termed the fiancé visa. This one allows you to move to and live in the USA. The downside, or upside, depending upon your point of view I suppose is that you need to marry someone within ninety days of arrival. Given I was pretty certain Paula was coming with me, and I didn't know anybody except our gay friend Kevin in the USA, it was difficult to see how this one would apply unless we were all willing to make significant sacrifices to the manner in which we currently lived our lives.

Then there are the E-type visas. These are employer-sponsored visas and are only available to employees with priority or exceptional skills. A visa of this type *was* a possibility for me. The problem is that, like many things in life, such good things often come with strings attached. The Immigrant E visa comes with weighty requirements from the State Department in that the employer must submit substantial proofs and due diligences that the same employee with the same skills, or similar, cannot be found in the United States before they are granted. That means that it can be more difficult to push through an already arduous and lengthy process.

Then there are the 'Golden' visas and the famous 'Lottery.'

The EB-5, or Golden visa is brilliant if you can get it, but, again, it comes with a few of those pesky minor strings attached. You must invest at least $800,000 in a US enterprise and create at least ten American jobs. Given we were short by about $790,000 and weren't going to employ anybody, this one looked to be a bit of a stretch.

The Lottery is more formally known as the Diversity Immigrant Visa. Its goal is to add diversity to the immigrant population in the United States. Around 13 million people apply annually from countries where, historically, there has been a low number of immigrants. It's a lottery because out of the 13 million applicants, only 55,000 immigrant visas are actually granted each year. The only way to be in with a chance of securing this one would be to first migrate from the UK to Cameroon or Uzbekistan and apply from there. This option also looked to be unlikely.

Non-immigrant visas include the F-1 or M-1 visas. These visas are reserved for full-time international students. They are only made available after the student has been offered and accepted by a school certified in the Student and Exchange Visitor Program. I hated school and I wasn't going back just to get a visa.

We decided that the best approach would be the L-1 visa. This is an employment visa for an intra-company transferee. To qualify for this category, any individual must have been employed by the same employer abroad, continuously, for at least one year within the three preceding years. The downside was that this visa was a non-immigrant visa, but at the time we only ever foresaw staying for a couple of years, three tops, so it seemed ideal.

For any visa option, obtaining one can be an extremely complicated, lengthy, and costly exercise for which it is highly recommended that you use the services of an experienced immigration lawyer.

For those contemplating such a thing, the process is broadly as follows and hopefully provides an insight into what you can expect. The first thing you get very used to is waiting for nothing much to happen, for a very extended period of time.

First off, the applicant's prospective employer must first obtain a labor certification approval from the Department of Labor. Once received, the employer then files an Immigrant Petition for Alien Worker, Form I-140, with the U.S. Citizenship and Immigration Services (USCIS) for the appropriate employment-based preference category.

These are the categories listed above, E-1, E-2, etc. If this step is approved and the visa category is agreed upon, the applicant then has to submit all required paperwork (Form DS-260), passport, photos, and proof of ability to financially support oneself through the visa time period. You then have to attend a medical examination and take all required vaccinations and then apply for, and go through, a face-to-face visa interview in their local US Embassy. If you manage to convince the immigration official that you have more than fifty quid in your bank account, are not currently working for Vladimir Putin, or an active member of Al Qaeda, several months later you will receive your passport back with the valuable visa stapled somewhere in the opening pages.

It is far from an easy process and each step can take months, so I found it hard to believe that this had somehow slipped John's mind. I was a bit annoyed with John's recommendation that we just move out and then a job would magically transpire, as he must have gone through the process to get one of the above, either the L visa or more likely the E category visa himself. I was beginning to suspect that the route to employment on John's team was going to be a non-starter.

Luckily, I had another meeting with a guy I had never met but had spoken to on many occasions. His name was Carel and I immediately got a more positive vibe. He had got approval to put a new team together. They were going to be a kind of special 'A-Team' for the Americas, to include South America and Canada. The team would be a total of four individuals, including Carel himself, all tasked with picking up the biggest, ugliest, and most technically problematic software installations we had sold, and had subsequently failed to get working correctly. The team's job would be to analyze the way the solutions were designed, recommend fixes, and make the customers were happy so that they would buy more of our shoddy software. So that we could then fail to get that to work correctly. It sounded like the sort of job where you could be employed forever without ever worrying about losing employment, like being a painter on the Forth Road Bridge or being a member of the British Royalty.

I assumed Carel would be the John "Hannibal" Smith of the group, a Texan guy called Doug would play Templeton "Faceman" Peck, somebody I hadn't yet met called Mike would be B. A. Baracus and they still needed a fourth to play "Howlin' Mad" Murdock. That would hopefully be me.

We chatted about the job for about an hour and then met the sales VP and we all went out for lunch together. We all hit it off and an informal job offer was extended. Success.

I drove back to Bahama Breeze to share the good news. I hadn't had the chance to call Paula to let her know that I had already eaten, and so she had taken advantage of the bar to sample a cocktail or three. She was starving when I arrived and a tad on the wobbly side, so we drove back to the Alpharetta highway and found a Mexican place called Taqueria San Pancho, whose menu was entirely in Spanish. She ordered by pointing at the menu board behind the counter, and when her order came it appeared to be 'greasy sinews of wild beast in a wrap (with beans)'. She took a bite and dumped the rest in a waste can in the car park. With a queasy stomach, we drove back to the hotel.

For our last dinner on our final night, we walked back across the road to Bahama Breeze and had a couple of ice-cold beers. We sat outside on the patio watching the sun dip beneath the tall buildings that clustered around the mall. Late-night shopper's whizzed past on the still busy highway. We had come to realize that most American patios are primarily about the need to park the diners' cars conveniently. The patios all face the car park and the road. In Europe, the car park will be located at the front of the restaurant by the road. The patio however, where the diners enjoy dinner, will be found to the rear, strategically placed to point its customers at a slow flowing, duck dappled river or a distant snow-capped mountain, or something else pleasant and distracting. There could be a prairie of stampeding buffalo out back of an American restaurant and the patio would still have you facing the road noise and pollution.

But it was still a very pleasant end to our visit. The heat of the day blew through the fine hairs on my forearms and lily-white legs. The beers were huge and icy cold, served in frosted mugs. Gigantic American flags still fluttered from the tops of tall buildings, like signal pennants on a spinnaker. The food was plentiful, the service was wonderful and the sound of the Caribbean music from the loudspeakers completed the illusion.

"Well, what do you think? Could you live here?" I asked.

Paula was quiet for some considerable time as she took in the clear skies, slowly darkening to the color of a vast shimmering glass of shiraz.

The stars were just beginning to poke their brilliance through the firmament.

"There's nothing here I don't think I couldn't tolerate," she answered.

And with that faint praise, our fates were sealed.

BACK TO ATL

A fter our overnight flight, we arrived back in the UK fatigued and jet lagged but still, we stayed up late and talked long into the night. There was a lot on the line and much for us to discuss. We had lived our entire lives in this one town. Neither one of us had ever lived anywhere else, even within the UK. We decided on a two-pronged approach. We could initiate the process and get the paperwork moving, without incurring too much cost to the company and too much commitment on our part to actually go through with the move. The other prong would be to visit Atlanta again, but this time take the kids with us to see what they thought about a new life in the United States.

So, we began the process. I filled out form after form and took photocopies of everything. We all queued at one of those photo booths outside Southport railway station to get the family's passport photos taken, me shouting at the kids that if they pulled one more face and ruined another set of pictures, we would leave them both behind.

We sent our precious passports off by recorded delivery to the United States Consulate in London.

In the meantime, I kept in regular contact with Carel and began to liaise with a guy called Mike who would be our USA-based Human Resources point of contact. The company I worked for was both large and multinational, so I assumed the company had a process to follow, and standard forms and contracts to issue to employees. It soon became apparent to me that, although I knew that they had processed foreign workers before, they were making everything up on the fly. It was all very ad-hoc, and every question and query was followed by several days of silence, while everybody over the pond thought about what the right answer might be.

The company put me in touch with a London-based immigration lawyer and the paperwork was gradually, and at a snail's pace, processed. I have to admit, it was a deeply unnerving time. I had somehow put myself in the strange position of still being actively busy with my job in the UK, working for the same boss who knew I was trying to leave, and meeting the same customers who were oblivious that, possibly, in a few months I would be gone from their projects and their lives. For the longest time, I found myself unwilling to commit to one path or the other. It was like walking a tightrope in a gale, having to carefully navigate the two career paths, making sure that I didn't lose my job in the UK, for what might turn out to be a fictitious role in the USA, all the while, and at the same time, making more and more almost accidental and incremental commitments to a life in the USA.

We agreed with Carel and Mike to a two-year visa with the option to extend to a third. The downside was that the UK office refused point blank to guarantee a role for me at the end of the visa period. If there was something suitable available when my time in the USA ran out, I was welcome to it, but if there wasn't...

Months slipped by with me chasing the lawyers in the UK and, in the USA, for Mike and Carel to put together a contract and a relocation package. At times it looked like it would all just be too problematic, and then, out of the blue we would take a giant single step forward and things would all be back on track again.

We took the kids to Atlanta for a week at the end of August, and very kindly Kevin put us up in one of his many spare rooms in his massive house in Roswell. To be honest, it was a little unfair of us, and during our stay, we sold a new life in the USA to Ben and Adam in a quite frankly outstandingly dishonest manner. We spent the days at amusement and water parks, we went to the Georgia Aquarium, (my that's a lot of fish); we even drove north and went fishing (more fish) for striper on Lake Lanier. We ate out every night, we all went bowling and later, we sat in massive reclining chairs in the cinema eating buckets of popcorn.

We took the cable car to the top of Stone Mountain and had hot buns thrown at us at Aunt Kate's, a diner modeled on a 19th-century frontier homestead which has sadly been replaced now by a modern burger joint. We watched a movie in 4D which, given we were in a relatively little-known backwater, was phenomenal. As well as the usual 3D on the screen, a bullfrog squirted us with actual water and fireflies tickled our ankles with fluttering tapes underneath our seats. We were blown away by the experience, of being so fully immersed in the tale of life in the Okefenokee swamp.

After Stone Mountain, we drove to Turner Field and parked up to watch our first-ever baseball game. As we walked through the gates some dude tried to take our picture so I shooed him away. In the UK this is always a sales scam, some inventive way to part you from your precious pounds. The man with the camera was quite insulted and quickly explained that the service was completely free and that the photos would be emailed to us. Free is my kind of price, snap away!

The game was fun but seemingly endless. We did enjoy all the games played to entertain the crowd between the innings, particularly Tool Race and the Kiss Cam. During the seventh-inning stretch we all stood to sing, "take me out to the ball game." It was so definitively American, and we loved every red, white, and blue second of it.

The heat of the afternoon was immense and we all sweated profusely, eating massive slices of pepperoni pizza like sword swallowers as the innings slipped slowly by. At the end of the game, they had an amazing, free fireworks display, explosions, and rockets scattered colored sparks across the sky, all set against the twinkling backdrop of downtown Atlanta. At the end, the crowd, mostly families, dispersed and we all walked back to our cars. The streets felt safe and were well-patrolled by the police. By the time we pulled out of the car park the kids were fast asleep. It was an incredible experience.

The next day we took a trip downtown to visit Atlanta Zoo, which for some original reason known only to the marketing team, they had decided to call Zoo Atlanta. We had a lovely time, but it was there that we all had our first experience of a weather system in the deep south of the United States. It had been a glorious day but extremely hot and ridiculously humid, particularly for a family more acclimated to a frigid drizzle and a damp mist. As we walked around the zoo, heavy, rain-filled cumulonimbus darkened the skies and, in the distance, we could hear the distant, constant rumble of thunder.

We hadn't noticed, but by the time we got to the chimpanzee enclosure, the zoo had slowly emptied around us. We stood alone looking through the fencing at the chimps who were scattered around their open-air space, seated on rocks and doing chimp things. The first thing we noticed was the faint tang of ozone on the tongue and then all hell broke loose. A sudden bolt of lightning struck the metal roof on a seating area not six feet from where we were all standing. There was a deafening and sustained 'CRAAAAAAAK' sound, and at the same time the very personal sensation that all of our skeletons were suddenly visible, lit from within by a crackling blue light. We looked around us in shock to see that all of the chimpanzees had disappeared, scattered for their lives, and we were left alone, the tallest things still standing amid the sudden onset of the electrical storm.

We started running just as the cloud ruptured and emptied its cold contents on us like some giant emptying a bathtub on our heads. In seconds we were as drenched as if we had been swimming in the ocean. We took due note that in the future we should respect these pop-up summer storms and seek shelter more readily.

At no time did we talk about a new school, having to make new friends, waiting for school buses, or needing vaccinations. For the last few days, we flew first class to New York and did all of the touristy things and then flew home from JFK. We all had a wonderful time and the boys simply couldn't wait to live more of this amazing American high life.

Even then, as we landed back in the UK at the beginning of September, I wasn't certain we could pull the relocation off. Six months had breezed by and the embassy paperwork was still outstanding and, while I had seen several emails from Mike making suggestions as to relocation packages and salaries, it was not a contract, something against which you could move your family internationally against.

The contract looked like it was going to be the most difficult to overcome. Never having done this before I had no idea what was fair, but I knew we would need a place to stay for a few months, a rental car, and a salary that would provide healthcare benefits. I didn't even really know what a fair salary would look like, so we ended up negotiating rather blindly.

And then, as these things often do, time that had long been slowed to an almost standing point suddenly accelerated into a manic panic. Our immigration lawyer emailed us with a date to visit the US Embassy in London for our formal interview. A few days later I received a draft of the contract from Mike. The job opening would start on January 1st, 2007.

The contract, in the end, looked good to me. The company offered us three months in a rental in Alpharetta, three months rental of a car, one full-size shipping container shipped from the UK to a named location in the USA, and free storage for up to one year for possessions we didn't want to move across to the USA. They even offered us two paid flights home for the first two years. And as far as I could tell, when adjusted for exchange rates, the salary was at least comparable to what I was making in the UK.

If you are considering such a move, I think this is a good template of what should be negotiated for. Obviously, it will depend massively on your existing position in the company. I was a manager of a small team at the time, so not particularly senior. I think on balance, it was a solid and very fair offer for me at that point in my career. If you are a CEO, you will likely be writing the contract yourself so good job you! Enjoy that penthouse apartment and Dodge Viper when you get there.

It's funny, even as an adult, how you lightly plan and make decisions that might irrevocably change your life. While you are in the process of planning it seems almost dreamlike and ethereal. Something removed from daily responsibilities and perhaps unlikely to ever *really* happen. And then somebody puts a contract in your hands. Suddenly I had a start date, a location, a contract, and a salary in hand. Our quiet and fairly normal life was about to be disrupted in a way that, over a year ago, over one too many glasses of wine, we could never have imagined. I suddenly needed to visit the bathroom quite urgently.

A Parachute

So now here we were. Only a little more than three months away from the date I was due to start work in the USA. Bloody hell—how had we suddenly got ourselves into this situation? It wasn't that we didn't want to go. We did. And the time for second thoughts had long passed us by. But the pure number of things that we needed to achieve in such a short time frame was massively overwhelming, which I think, looking back now, was a very good thing indeed. It felt as if we had stepped from a sedate country railway platform and boarded the bullet train. Our destination was distant but there was only one stop and we were going to get there rather quickly whether we liked it or not.

I liken the feeling to the one day, a few years before our move, when I did a parachute jump out of a plane for charity. We trained all day, climbing out of a rudely and roughly made wooden model of a Cessna plane that sat on the ground by the jump school. We all shuffled out along the board that sat above the landing wheel, one at a time, all holding onto the wing strut and waiting for the jump controller to give us the thumbs up, before jumping backward to land on the ground three feet below us shouting, "one-one-thousand, two-one-thousand, check canopy". Practicing with the ground three feet below me was easy.

Later that same day, in the actual plane, at a cow shrinkingly 4,000 feet, when my turn to jump came, I was rendered entirely numb. I was an automaton. I willingly climbed out of the safety of the fuselage and into the gale of velocity-generated wind. I shuffled my toes out along the board, holding onto only the wing strut for support, a veritable chasm of death below my feet. I looked back, eyes wide into the fuselage to see the jump controller give me a smiling thumbs up, and without a moment's thought, I jumped backward, trusting my life to a distracted parachute packer I had never met, who probably earned less than minimum wage.

I plummeted in a way I had never plummeted before. Or since. And I sincerely hope never to plummet in such a manner ever again. I didn't look back up at the plane or arch my back and stretch my arms and legs out to become aerodynamically stable as I had been instructed. I adopted more of a flailing, rolling, head over heels, arse over tit approach to the whole thing.

I also didn't shout, "one-one-thousand, two-one-thousand, check canopy." It was much more something akin to "holy fucking shiiii-iiiiiiiiiiiit," before the jolt from the straps, as the parachute opened, roused me back into something with an almost functioning brain. Well, I can honestly attest that those final weeks before we moved were just like that feeling.

Our date for the meeting with US immigration was only a few days distant so I booked return train tickets to London and the day off work. Now we had to decide what to do with the house.

Lots of people we have met over the last few years, who either preceded our move, or came after us, chose to rent out their homes in the UK, particularly when the plan all along had been to do two, perhaps three years at the most in the USA and then return. That made perfect sense, very logical. So, of course, we thought we would do something different.

We decided to sell and rebuy in the States. One of the reasons was to truly experience life in a different country. When we had visited Atlanta with the kids only a few weeks ago we had got dinner at a friend's house. His name was Nick and his wife was Linda. They were just completing two years working in the States and were preparing to return back to the UK. They had rented out their home in the UK and had found a rental in the USA. The house we visited was in Cumming, a few exits further north than where we really wanted to be. It was nice enough, but none of it felt like a real home. It was furnished like a rental, decorated like a rental, and felt like what it was—temporary.

They always intended on returning to the UK, to their home. They were quite posh and financially better off than us. Their children were quite young and as their children got older, they wanted access to better, private schools to further their education. Our kids were in state-run schools in the UK already, and not particularly good ones at that, unless you wanted to learn how to spit really far and fight bare knuckle. Anything the USA could offer was likely to be an improvement for them.

In the USA, Nick and Linda lived in a community of other renters, many of whom were also British. It was like a posh version of Crossroads but where nobody knew anybody else or had made any real friends outside of work. It wasn't what we wanted at all. If we were going to do this, we wanted to live amongst Americans, make some

American friends, and become part of a community, one we chose to settle in.

Nick and Linda were lovely but they were quintessentially British, slim, pale, and terrified of all things American, especially the wildlife. Linda kept all the doors sealed constantly, squeezing through any external door held open the bare minimum, presumably to keep out the snakes, bears, and coyotes that lurked with ill intent in the bushes outside. Linda did give us some good advice. When we asked what the winters were like in Atlanta, Linda told us not to bother bringing coats or jumpers, it seldom fell below sixty degrees and a light jacket and shorts were all that would be needed.

So, we put the house on the market and waited for an offer while we tackled the next big problem—what to ship and what to leave behind. Of course, all of our precious electrical items would have to be sold or placed into storage, the voltage and outlets being completely different in the USA. Finally, I had a valid excuse to buy a big-screen plasma TV when we got there.

Pretty much everything else we would take with us. For some reason, which is still a mystery to me, the exception to this was the set of steps and a full-size set of extending ladders I owned. I don't know why I thought that all things 'up' would not be a problem in America but leave them behind we did. Based on Linda's advice we also put aside all of our bulky and warm clothing. That could all follow us on the ship, along with all of our furniture, kitchenware, and odds and ends on the container, which would be shipped slowly across the Atlantic to join us later.

By far our biggest logistical challenge was to find a way to safely transport Bandit and Scout and Tinky Winky. The pups had become aware that changes were afoot. They saw us sorting through our belongings, and placing things into piles. Things to take in suitcases, things for the container, things to place into storage, and crap to get rid of. They had begun to follow us around wondering which pile they would end up in. At the same time Paula started to look into pet transport companies and, after deliberating a thousand options, we agreed on a plan of logistics.

I would fly out on the 2nd of January 2007, pick up the rental car at the airport, and get the keys to the apartment. I would then be at the apartment to take receipt of the animals that Paula would have dropped off in airport secure crates at customs, in Manchester, the day after my arrival. Paula and the boys would then take a flight themselves the following day, in time for me to pick them up from Hartsfield Jackson Airport.

We were put in touch with a UK moving company that had been subcontracted by Peachtree Movers who were Atlanta-based. The UK company gave us moving crates and we started packing.

The meeting in London with the Embassy was a stressful day of waiting. Top tip. On your visit take a book, 'War and Peace' or anything written by Salman Rushdie, anything really, but make it hefty and distracting.

It was the first time I had been inside of any embassy building and I was very excited. Everything I knew about such places I had gleaned from watching James Bond films and Ferrero Rocher adverts, sparkling chandeliers, sumptuous furniture, flutes of champagne handed out by beautiful waitresses who might, or might not be who they presented themselves to be. So, the disappointment, after we passed through security, was quite profound.

They placed us amid fifty or sixty other groups of couples, all on arse numbingly hard chairs in an airless and undecorated room, all nervously fingering the packets of forms and documents we had been tasked to bring to the interview. I am certain the ambassador and his cohorts all lived in splendor behind one of the oak doors that led from the room we were in, but the aesthetic here shouted, "we are the fricking USA, we have eagles and guns and shit so, if you want some of what we got, show some fricking patience and humility."

The wait was interminable. It's part of the problem with having a surname that starts with a W. All of my life I had been last to be picked, called upon, and given results to, and the American embassy was no exception. It did give us an early insight into the tedium and pointlessness of US bureaucracy though. One by one the groups were called to step through a hallway and disappear for between ten and twenty minutes. First, the Browns were called, and then the Crawfords, the Denbighs, and the Fernbottoms. Minutes and hours ticked by. Lunch was missed and then the Havefords were called. There was a long delay while the Guptas were called into the interrogation, sorry, interview room, but they came out smiling and happy enough. The room slowly emptied.

It was close to four in the afternoon when the Vince family's name was called. I was thinking we might have to get a hotel and spend an unplanned night in London, but then, last of all in the empty room, our name was shouted and we rose with stiff limbs and numbed buttocks. We walked nervously into the interview room. The official looked as bored with his job as we were fatigued by waiting for him to do it. He thumbed through our paperwork and asked us inane questions like:

"Why do you want to live in the USA?"

"How long do you think you will be there for?"

"Have you ever been part of the Taliban?"

He nodded at our equally inane answers and then stamped three or four forms with a very official-looking stamp that bore the image of an eagle, wings widespread. We were done; the application was accepted.

Planning

We picked up our passports that now bore the smart-looking L-1 visa stapled within, from our immigration lawyers on another trip to London, and we put our minds to trying to put the fine details on the plan.

We had an offer on the house and that all seemed to be falling into place quite nicely. It was still the plan for me to leave Paula and the kids to finish packing and fly out on the 2nd of January. After making sure that the pets were safely at the airport her sister would pick her and the kids up on the 4th of January and they would follow me, leaving our solicitors to finalize the sale.

I started thinking about credit cards and bank accounts. My first thought was to try and open a US-based bank account while I was still in the UK. Of course, that is an absolute non-starter. You need to be able to prove you have a USA-based permanent address. I called up HSBC, you know, the 'Global Bank', and asked if I was to take out a UK account and card it would then be transferrable to the States. The guy at HSBC almost laughed in my face. I am certain it was the first time he had even been asked for such an extraordinary thing. The only people who had a clue were American Express. They were fairly sure, not certain, but somewhat confident, that if I took out a UK account, although it wouldn't allow me to transfer my credit rating across, it would expedite the application and opening of a USA-based account.

The reality is that even though there are strong trade and tax agreements between the UK and the USA, as an individual there is no way to transfer your hard-won credit rating in either direction. On the day that you wash up on that foreign shore you are viewed in the same way that a newborn might be, bereft of financial history and worth. I started to think that, like Jack Reacher or a gang of Columbian drug runners, we would need to be carrying cash for quite some time.

The next thing on our minds was somewhere to live when we arrived in the USA. Mike from HR had sent across a list and brochures for some company-approved apartments that they were willing to pay for on our behalf for the first three months. They were all three-bedroom corporate apartments which meant that they would all be furnished. It's one of the great things that the US does better than the UK, there are lots of apartment complexes in the major cities and they serve a broad spectrum of budgets. Trying to get a rental in the UK can be next to impossible, particularly on a short-term let.

We picked one that at the time was called AMLI at Northpoint. It was close to the mall and the office and not too far from the Embassy Suites hotel we had stopped at earlier in the year when we first began checking Atlanta out as a place to live. The complex had tennis courts and a gym. There was even a restaurant within walking distance. It all looked clean and tidy and well-located.

Because the company was paying for the accommodation there was no paperwork for us to complete, but I did have to negotiate (fight) to have the lease written out in my name. If you are considering a similar move, this is something you *must* do. That lease, printed up with your legal name, and matching your passport, will be needed for all sorts of fun things when you arrive. Without it, such necessities as bank accounts and social security cards will long be denied to you.

We had a farewell party back at a venue called the Rookery in late November. The Rookery was attached to a cricket club and for a small joining fee you got access to cheap beer and a sticky dance floor, all within easy walking distance of where we all lived. It had been the venue of all of the major events of our lives. All of our baby showers, christenings, birthdays, weddings, anniversaries, divorces, funerals, and the occasional New Year's Eve party. The leaving party was fancy dress and a great opportunity to say goodbye to all of our friends.

It was a wonderful night. All of our family were there of course, but lots of friends we hadn't seen for many years also turned up to say farewell. I was dressed as 'Braveheart' and had a wig to match. I didn't take it off all night and could be seen flicking the hair out of my eyes, something I hadn't done since I was nineteen. They had to tear it from my hands the next day to return it to the hire shop.

A good friend of mine from high school even turned up. He had moved out of the area after school and we hadn't seen each other since. He had just moved back to Southport and was hoping we could get together for a pint now and again. His face was a picture when he found out it was our leaving do and we would be living abroad, in America, in only a few short weeks.

The most stressful thing about the move was our pets. The company wouldn't help with them so it was all down to us. When I say us, what I really mean is Paula. The logistics are simply insane but somehow, she figured it all out.

Something everybody still asks us is, do the dogs and cats need to stay in quarantine for four months. The short answer is no. The longer answer is that it all depends on if you get the paperwork correct and follow and meet all of the guidelines.

To move a pet from the UK to the USA is relatively simple, but it is good to know the requirements in both directions as many people do end up returning. The USA requires no permits and no rabies certificate as the UK and Ireland are rabies-free. But you do need a health certificate from your veterinarian stating that your pet is fit and healthy to travel and the animals must be microchipped. At the time we used pet passports to expedite the process but these have been discontinued since the UK left the European Union.

The rules for moving pets back to the UK are much more restrictive than going from the UK to the USA. To move a pet (dog, cat, or for some strange reason, ferret) back to the UK you must:

Have the animal microchipped, have a pet passport or health certificate, been vaccinated against rabies, use an approved route - unless you're traveling from Ireland, and fill out a declaration that you are not going to sell or transfer the ownership of your pet. Dogs must also have a tapeworm treatment within a few days of travel.

If you fail to follow these guidelines and meet the time limits inherent in many of the steps, this is when your pet may be put into quarantine for up to four months, or even simply refused entry if you arrived by sea.

And don't forget. Be very careful if, while in the USA (or any other overseas territory), that if you decide to buy a dog while you are there, and then subsequently want to return to the UK, it must not be one of the banned breeds such as the Pit Bull Terrier, Japanese Tosa, Dogo Argentino or Fila Brasileiro. In addition to not being specifically one of the restricted breeds banned by the UK Government, it must not *resemble* or have any characteristics of those breeds. If it does, and the government official determines that it is too close a match it could be destroyed.

If you can afford it, do use the services of an international animal courier. In fact, some airlines are now making this mandatory. If you use such a service, they will want you to use their 'airline-approved' animal cages, for which they will charge you a hefty premium. If you choose to supply your own crate, which is perfectly acceptable, you must ensure they meet or exceed the minimum requirements stipulated by your airline. Get this right! If you make an error and nobody picks it up, they will be refused travel. You can also expect to be asked, again and again, by your pet courier to confirm that you have not made a mistake when measuring and weighing your pets.

Measure five times and ship once is the adage here. Requirements sometimes differ when you travel in different directions, UK to USA or USA to UK, even if you travel on the same airline.

Weigh kitty and puppy (and ferrety if you have one) accurately, follow the guidelines for measuring height and length, take photos if you can against the measurements, and write them all down. You will be questioned again and again on how accurately you did these measurements, make sure you did it correctly and document it.

The best advice I could give, having done this several times now, is just to wait for little Rover to gently pass away in peace and bury him beneath the sod of the land he was born in. Mark their passing, if you have to, with a cross made from ice-lolly sticks, and then you can proceed to make your plans. I really can't stress it enough, if you love your pets like we do, the most worrying, time-consuming and money separating part of moving internationally is dealing with your beloved cuddle bunnies.

A New Home

We had a last family Christmas in our little house on Sussex Road, in Southport. Many of our possessions were already packed, and boxes and cases littered hallways and spare rooms. I sold my car to one of those companies that will pick it up for free for precisely half of what it is worth, but I needed to get rid of it and at that point, we were now in the frenzy of a panicked rush.

Because I was doing an intra-company transfer, I didn't have to hand in my cellphone or laptop, and in the preceding weeks, I had been busy at meetings saying farewell to all of the customers I had built friendships with over the last five or six years. It was all quite emotional and I got lots of sweet goodbye and good-luck emails from those I wouldn't have the chance to say farewell to in person.

Christmas passed and then we were facing our last New Year's Eve. We partied with friends and family at the Rookery social club. And then, finally, the day of the move was upon us.

The eight months and more of planning and deliberating over every decision, the precipitous highs and the depressing lows, the crushing disappointments and heart-fluttering excitements. The worries and the laughs. They were all nearly over. The very next morning I had to get a cab to Manchester airport and fly to Atlanta on my own. I was thrilled, and at the same time, I felt torn in two. I was leaving Paula and the boys behind to deal with the movers, organizing the safe shipping of Bandit, Scout and Tinky Winky, the closing of the house, and getting themselves to the airport for their flight to America.

In the morning I woke early and packed the last of what I would take with me. I had two large cases along with my backpack and I stood at the front room window, sipping a cup of hot tea in the half light of the morning waiting for the car I had booked to come and pick me up. Those butterflies were really fluttering. Our little house, our home was nearly empty. The walls we had decorated, the kitchen we had renovated, the rooms we had celebrated Christmases and birthdays in, births and deaths, crying and laughing together. Even the house, the bricks and the mortar, felt like they were waiting, like an inhalation, for the next jagged breath of the journey.

It is that pivotal moment you have destined and crafted for yourself. That 'you' of the past, the one that wanted this and planned all of this, the one that didn't care that it would be the future 'you' who would have to deal with all of this stress and sudden action. You wanted it, you planned for it, and now, despite all of your reservations that suddenly come flooding in on a tide that cannot be turned, it sucks at your feet and moves the mud underneath your feet to pull you inexorably, deeper and deeper into that fast-moving river.

The taxi finally pulled up and I gave Bandit and Scout a cuddle, hugged the kids tight, and with a voice constricted by emotion, kissed and said goodbye to Paula. It felt to me at the time that I faced much more than a day or two of separation. It felt like I was being taken away to be incarcerated or sent to war, a gut wrench, a punch to the solar plexus. I dumped my cases in the boot of the car and took my seat in the back. Paula and the kids came out to stand, shivering against the cold of the New Year, on the rain-slicked pavement outside the house. The curtains of the neighbors twitched as we waved our goodbyes. The next time I would see my little family again would be in a new and very different country. Finally, the car pulled slowly away, and from the rear window, I watched as they receded as the distance between us grew. Then the car turned the corner and the house and our familiar street retreated out of sight. No going back.

The first step away is always the hardest one, but once set in motion the only option left is to continue to take those steps, small cautious ones initially, but then with more confidence and vigor, until they become long and eager strides towards that next goal.

The flight was long and uneventful. I was seated next to a young American guy who was traveling home to Atlanta. We started chatting and when he found out I was on my flight to begin a new life in his city. He was hugely intrigued and asked me a ton of questions. I had quite a few of my own. The one theme we kept coming back to was the amount, and deadly toxicity of, the myriad snake varieties that lay in my near future. Apparently, according to him, at least, Copperheads, Rattlers, and Cottonmouths roamed freely through gardens and homes, lying in wait, fangs dripping venom, for the incautious to tread too close.

We landed around five in the afternoon. The sun was already low in a sky filled with clouds. I got off the flight and tested the validity of the visa with a nervous grin at border security. The uniformed officer thumbed through my passport with a look of boredom on his stern face until he came across the visa. He paused and took a second to look up at me properly for the first time.

"Welcome home sir," he said as he handed the passport back to me.

It blew my mind. Out of all of the myriad things we had done and accomplished over the span of almost a year, it all came crashing down and reality rushed up to greet me. This was it; like it or not, this was my new home.

I picked up my luggage at the carousel and wheeled the cases awkwardly across the bumps of the terminal towards the automatic doors at the exit. Taking Linda's advice, all of my coats and jumpers would be shortly in a container headed for the Atlantic crossing, so it was with some dismay that I stepped outside into a stiff wind so frigid it immediately stiffened my nipples and grimaced my teeth. I stood there looking like the dog in the back of the truck in Planes, Trains and Automobiles muttering, "fuck you, Linda."

Luckily for me, back in 2007, the car rental station was located just across the road from the terminal (it's now a shortish train journey on the MARTA) and I was quickly ensconced, with the heater blasting, in the red Suzuki Vitara that had been arranged for me. I set up my Tom Tom sat nav and entered the address for the AMLI apartments. I knew I would be arriving too late for the rental office to still be open so had called them the day before, and they had promised to leave the key and gate opener under the mat, outside the office door, which I thought, for America, was very trusting and sweet.

Traffic on I-85 was hellish, as always, and it took me close to an hour to find the exit off GA-400 for Haynes Bridge Road. I made a left and then a right onto Westside Parkway. I saw the turn for the apartments but needed something to eat so carried straight on to where I knew there was a Publix supermarket.

Inside the supermarket, I wandered around for fifteen minutes looking in vain for something that might resemble a dinner for one that I could quickly heat up. There are a thousand options in the UK to allow single, sad, and lonely men to feed themselves, but I was dog tired, barely awake and I couldn't find anything in the unfamiliar layout of the store. I walked the endless aisles, up and down and back again. In the end, I was seduced by the picture of a carton with a large burger filled with pulled pork on a box that shouted, "MANWICH." I picked up a bottle of red wine, an old vine zinfandel that looked like it would add suitable tasting notes to the fancy meal, and headed to the checkouts.

With eyes fluttering closed and the fatigue and prolonged stress of the day really hitting me hard, I got back in the car and finally turned, with a huge sigh of relief, into the parking lot of the AMLI. Thankfully, the key and opener were where they had promised to leave it and I drove around the units trying, in the darkness, to find the correct apartment block. It took me a couple of circuits, jet-lagged as I was, to figure out the numbering scheme, and after parking the car, another ten minutes to figure out that our apartment was down some steps, but I finally found the right one and jiggled the key to open the door and dragged my tired bones and two heavy cases inside.

Too tired to even check out the apartment fully, I turned on the TV, and microwaved my Manwich, which turned out, despite the image on the packaging, to not include a hamburger bun, it was just a big pile of seasoned meat or what I would soon learn to call a 'Sloppy Joe', opened my bottle of wine and sat on the sofa, shoveling Joe's sloppy meat into my mouth and watching The Last Samurai movie on TV until I could keep my eyes open no longer.

A First Morning

I woke wondering where on earth I was. The bed and ceiling were unfamiliar and I sat up with a start. And then the entire previous day came crashing back down on me. I was in America. And I was living here. This was my new home.

The day was bright and the skies were clear and full of promise. I had a quick look around the apartment and was really pleased with the choices we had made. I called Paula to let her know that I was safe and everything looked OK. She was just about to set off to the pet customs area at Manchester airport and was pretty stressed out and upset, so I made it short and sweet. I too had a stressful and busy day ahead of me.

There is an order in which you must do things if you ever feel the need to move to the United States. In many ways, it is a truly wonderful country, but it is one of the world's great bureaucracies. One of the most critical items you must have is a social security card and number. Without it, you simply do not exist. Its primary function is that it gives you the right to work. For such an important document it is strange indeed that it comes in the form of a small, credit card-sized piece of paper, easy to stain and tear and lose.

The hard truth is that without that little piece of unlaminated paper, with its unique number, you really can't get very far in any aspect of everyday life in the USA. Every utility company, phone company, credit bureau, bank, and store will ask you for it, and if you can't provide it, the script ends in an abrupt, "well then sir, I just caiiint help y'all."

This morning I hoped to achieve two things. First, was that I wanted to try and open a bank account, of which my hopes of success were admittedly low. The reason I was not hopeful was that item number two was to drive to the Social Security office and apply for a social security card which I suspected I would need to open the bank account. The reason I didn't go the Social Security office first was that the bank was close, just across the road, and even if I was successful at the Social Security office, the card would take weeks before it would be issued.

I made some coffee and stepped outside in the jeans and T-shirt Linda had told me was all that I would need in Atlanta. The car was covered in a layer of ice thick enough to skate on, and the wind that shrieked from the north numbed trembling knees and bloodless fingers as I scraped away the ice to form two little peepholes with my shiny, new, and useless UK American Express card.

"Fuck you Linda," I muttered to myself.

I had in my little transparent document pouch the rental agreement, passport, visa, and a plethora of other documents I thought I might be questioned about or had the potential value to help me conclude business; birth certificates, wedding certificate, cycling proficiency certificate and a badge I won in junior school for swimming the twenty-five meters breaststroke. I had *all* of the bases covered.

I chose Bank of America for no good reason other than the branch was nearby and there seemed to be a subtle clue in the name. The alternative was called Fifth Third Bank and having been pretty good at fractions in high school, I didn't quite trust a bank that didn't seem capable of doing sums, with my money.

I parked the car and walked into the branch with my little bundle of documents in hand. There were a few people already queuing at the teller desk and the glass doors to the offices were all closed, so I stood looking English, clueless and entirely out of my depth in the middle of the vestibule. Luckily for me, the branch manager, a lovely lady called Jennifer saw me through the glass door of her office, took pity, and came out to help me.

"What can I do for you hun?"

"I need to open a bank account if I may."

She made a little squeal of delight, "oh well bless your heart, you're English aint ya?"

"I am indeed, how did you tell?"

"Oh sweety, your accent is just a-dor-a-ble! Come on in my office and we'll get you all sorted out. Let me get you and me a coffee first."

She walked over to the counter by the door where a large pot of coffee was waiting, brewed and fresh and free for the use of its customers. A pile of cookies lay on a tray to the side. For the first time, I took a moment to look around me and take in the affluence of my surroundings. Polished stainless steel and floor-to-ceiling glass dominated the open space. Comfortable bright blue couches and easy chairs were scattered around for the use of waiting customers. A rack of new magazines and newspapers were available for those inconvenienced enough to have to wait a few minutes for an appointment.

This was very far from what I was used to. English banking establishments generally aim for a mix of Victorian austerity and authoritarianism, but seldom manage to resemble anything more than the inside of a frugal and rude Dickensian workhouse. If you have seen any of the Harry Potter movies, believe me when I tell you that J. K. Rowling didn't have to use too much of her prodigious imagination to portray the goblins or interior at Gringotts Bank, she just needed to try and make a cash deposit at a high street branch of the Bank of England, and there she would have found all of the characters and surroundings waiting, fully written for her.

Sat in Jennifer's office, warming hands around the fresh coffee, I explained my situation, the fact that I had just arrived, and that I didn't have an SSN yet, but that was my next port of call and I would soon have one. She asked for the rental agreement, nodded, and tapped away on her computer and, shockingly, less than ten minutes later I was standing by my car, breath steaming in the cold clear day with a bank card and temporary cheques in hand.

Buoyed by this unexpected success I jumped back in the car and drove, close to an hour, to Kennesaw where the social security office was located. I was much more confident of achieving my goal here. The visa itself entitled me to work, getting the social security number should be a formality, but with American bureaucracy you can never quite be sure that you have all of the right paperwork in all of the right order. I parked the car all the way around the back of the building, which resembled, and had all of the charm of, a concrete 1970s nuclear bunker.

The interior was a surprise though. The inside much more resembled a 1914 World War One front-line army hospital. The walls were painted the shade of green intended to demoralize and subdue any enemy combatant. Rows upon rows of hard chairs were aligned across the open space, standing on carpet tiles so stained with some dark fluid, they wouldn't have looked out of place in an episode of NCIS.

All that was needed were a few chalk outlines of stabbing and gunshot victims to finish off the illusion.

On the chairs were seated the largest representative cross-section of humanity I have ever seen in a single location. A pearl-clutching lady who clearly lunched was seated, nose held high while dressed in a Luis Vitton dress next to a poor man in a wheelchair with a face turned deathly pale, wheezing oxygen from a tank at his side. A rough-looking couple holding a snotty and screaming baby looked in my direction, as did a middle-aged businessman with a neat mustache and a briefcase. Another young Latino dude with a shaved head and straggly beard stared at me with a look of pure hatred on his face. Skin tones of every hue, young and old, rich and destitute, all sat crowded together in the controlling and unhurried hands of the Federal Government.

I stopped a few feet inside the entrance to try and get my head around how this system operated, while I subconsciously secreted my expensive watch in a trouser pocket. Along the walls were arrayed little booths, the occupants of which, were protected by plexiglass. Each booth had a letter taped to the window. In the center of the room, a screen suspended from the ceiling scrolled a three-digit number. Next to each number was assigned a letter. Below the scrolling screen on a supporting column was an electronic machine with bright yellow buttons. I walked over and read the lengthy instructions. Then I read them again. It was like somebody in government was doing their best to try and communicate something to me but had decided to obfuscate the meaning by using ten words, where any single one would have sufficed.

I finally figured out that the buttons were assigned to the categories of the requirements that the office sought to satisfy. I found the category that included requesting a new social security number and pressed the associated button. A little ticket was printed and popped out of the slot. On it was my three-digit number. Now I just needed to find a seat safely away from the most dangerous and 'stabby' looking occupants of the chairs and stare nervously at the scrolling screen to wait for my number to be displayed.

It actually didn't take too long, not more than an hour, and then my number popped up and invited me to meet the government official at window K. I wouldn't say that the large black lady at window K was unfriendly as such, but she had clearly worked there for ten years too long, processing the same damn forms for the same depressed and sullen customers who passed by her little window every day.

I tried to be upbeat and chatty and really turned on the British accent until I sounded not unlike Hugh Grant in Notting Hill, I even threw in a "whoopsidaisies," for good measure, but she had passed far beyond my powers of charm to coerce and win over.

But I have to admit she was efficient and, despite my fears that I had neglected to bring one form or proof of something or other, she stamped the paperwork and finally looked up at me to drawl, "OK English, you SSN be in the post in no more than a month or more."

"Thank you," I said in cheery, plummy tones, smiling my widest smile.

"Hmmm, hmmm," she replied. I was dismissed.

Back in the car, the sat nav took me a different way back to Roswell as if to ensure I would never get my bearings. I stopped off at the huge liquor store near the apartment which was a really strange experience. I was so indoctrinated by American TV shows and Hollywood movies, the environment was immediately familiar to me even though it was my first time stepping inside one. The racks of coolers, the stacks of beer cartons, the neon signs advertising Coors Light and Budweiser, the high counter with the stereotypical liquor store worker stood behind. My senses tingled and I looked nervously at every new person who came in through the door. I was *certain* that in only a matter of moments, one of these people would pull out a gun and hold the place up. Of course, it never happened, everybody seemed to know that the guy behind the counter was packing too.

One of the nuances of the USA is its archaic liquor laws, not helped by the fact that they vary wildly by state. In Georgia when we first arrived, the supermarkets sold beer and wine but not spirits such as whisky and vodka. Hard liquor you had to buy in a liquor store such as the one I was in. On Sunday you couldn't buy booze of any kind at all. Again and again, I would walk to the checkouts in Publix with a bottle of wine in hand on a Sunday evening, only for the checkout lady to finger her crucifix, and tut at me as she rolled her eyes and shook her head. The fact that the lights were out in the booze section never once tipped me off.

After picking up some wine and gin, my next stop was the pet store to buy food and water bowls, and some kibble for the cat and the dogs who should be arriving in a few hours. I did a quick basics shop at the Publix I had shopped at the night before and then raced back to the apartment to wait for the animals.

I got back around five in the afternoon. Just in time to find out from the pet courier company we had employed, that the animals had arrived in Atlanta safe and sound, but that the customs officials who deal with the inspection and release of livestock had all gone home. Our beloved pets would just have to stay in kennels at the airport overnight, and the pet courier company promised to pick them up and deliver them to the apartment the next morning.

REUNITED

The weather remained bitterly cold outside. There was a strong wind from the north that rattled the frost-grimed trees behind the apartment. I yawned as I made tea in the kitchen the next morning. I couldn't run any additional errands that morning, as I was expecting the pets to be delivered and wasn't 100% sure at what time that might be. I walked across to where the bank of mailboxes was located for all of the apartments, hunched against the icy blast. I had been given a key and wanted to make sure we hadn't missed any important mail and to make doubly sure that I had given all of the correct details to Jennifer at the Bank of America and to the sassy lady with no name at the social security office.

The animals arrived in a van around ten-thirty and I helped the guy carry the crates into the apartment. Bandit was fine, he was the bigger and older Blenheim King Charles and, not being blessed with the sharpest of intellects, had been insulated from really understanding what was happening to him. He just seemed to be thirsty and after emptying a bowl or three of cold water he lay down on the couch and had a very long and extremely wheezy snooze.

Scout was less well. She was small, even for her age but sharp as a tack. She had clearly not enjoyed the flight, the extra overnight in kennels or the car ride north to the apartment. Stressed out, she had almost chewed and scratched through the plywood sides of her crate, terrified by the entire experience. I checked her teeth and claws and, thankfully, she hadn't done any lasting damage to herself. I sat on the couch next to Bandit, with Scout on my knee, tickling her under her tiny chin until she fell asleep on her back, legs in the air.

For some reason, that we never really understood, Tinky Winky (the ginger cat) took an immediate and irreversible dislike to America. Perhaps she could smell the coyotes in the woods that backed up to the apartment, or sense the snakes slithering around in the kudzu, but regardless, she refused to go outside. She seemed well enough and took food and water, there was just something that put her right off the entire country. She never got over it.

I made a sandwich but didn't really enjoy it, and I am a man who really enjoys a sandwich. Everything was far too sweet for my English tastes; both the Little Debbie bread and the Southern sliced ham both seemed to be loaded with sugar.

I called up American Express and explained that I needed to swap my UK account for a USA-based one. I got almost all the way through the script, and I was getting thrilled that I was going to add another success to the day, when the agent on the other end of the line asked me for my social security number. Darn it.

I spent some time sending some emails to Carel to let him know I was finally in the country and I set up a meeting in the office with IT, and then I had nothing to do but wait until Paula's flight got close. I sat mindlessly refreshing flight tracker on the Delta website to see where above the Atlantic Paula's flight was.

Mid-afternoon I set off for the airport to meet Paula and the boys. I had to use sat nav everywhere I went, both to get somewhere and then to get back again. I had literally no idea where I was or where I was going. It made me feel like a child and honestly, it was exhausting.

Americans seem to have a built-in compass and measure distances by days. Ask an American for directions to the nearest CVS and they will tell you, "oh, it's real close. Just head north by north-west for 200 miles. You will pass thirty-three McDonalds and then when you see Jersey Mike's turn southeast. Drive another 150 miles, across the state line and it will be right there on your left."

English people balk at driving more than 25 miles *anywhere*. But we do have more interesting directions to follow.

"Do you know where Doctor Horace Ramsbottom's office is?"

"Of course, it's only a three or four miles away. Just turn right at the Skewered Traitor and then follow that lane for two miles, go across two cattle grids until the lane changes to a single track. At the sign of the old mill, you know the one where that funny business with the vicar and the goat took place? Well, turn right there, and you'll pass the duck pond on the village green where they used to drown the witches. Well, when you come to the stocks and the Norman Chapel, you'll see the sign for the Slutten Wench. The Doctor's surgery will be next door."

And of course, by the time you get there, the accent will have changed twice and the locals will have a different name for bread rolls.

The road south was loaded with cars and trucks and buses as usual, and it took me well over an hour to complete the thirty-three-mile journey, but I was still early so I parked the car in the short-term parking lot and went into the terminal to wait.

I saw Paula's flight arrival announced on the arrival board but still had to wait a long time, peering through the lines of faces that slowly rose into view from the escalators that brought passengers up from the 'plane train' as it is now called.

Atlanta airport is the busiest in the world and one I would soon get to know a little too well. Back in 2007, when we arrived, both domestic and international passengers were all herded through the same departure/arrival gates and security lines. That same year, Hartsfield Jackson, or ATL as everybody calls it, handled 88 million passengers. In pre-pandemic years that number has gone as high as 110 million passengers. The capacity was alleviated slightly, and the international flying experience improved vastly, with the opening of a $1.4 billion terminal in 2012, provisioned solely for the departure and arrival of international customers.

Still scanning the faces, finally I saw them. Paula first and then Ben and finally Adam. They looked tired but were pleased to see me. We all hugged, picked up the cases from the always crowded and chaotic baggage reclaim, and stepped outside of the terminal to cross the road to get to the short-term parking lot. Paula and the kids had dressed, as I had, for a mild Atlanta winter, something in the mid-50s, perhaps. We all wore only pants and t-shirts so it was with some shock, especially after the nine-hour flight and the heat of the terminal building, to feel the blast of 25-degree Siberian air pimple bare arms and redden puckered faces.

"It's bloody freezing," said Paula through gritted teeth.

"I know, it's been like this all week."

"But all of our coats and stuff are on the container ship. Fuck you, Linda."

"That's what I said!"

Paula turned on the heat in the Suzuki and liked the car straight away, it was a good size, not too large. The drive back to the apartment was easy. I even knew where I was for a few minutes.

I held my breath as I opened the door to the apartment. If Paula hated it, we were in for a rough few months. But Bandit and Scout were waiting, wagging tails and jumping up, deliriously happy to see her and the boys again. Ben and Adam ran around like kids do, claiming bedrooms and turning on the TVs. Paula walked around slowly, opening doors and cupboards, and then checked out our bedroom. Her eyes lit up when she opened what she thought to be a dressing room door only to reveal a sparkling En-suite.

"I love it. It's great," she said.

We had never had an En-suite before. This was luxury for us.

Paula and the boys were travel weary, so for dinner we walked, in the dark, across the apartment complex, hunched, hands in pockets against the bitter cold, to the Village Tavern, the restaurant that was close to the apartment block. We sat in a darkened booth, trying to read the menu under the meager light on the table. Our young, and very southern waiter arrived and listened attentively and with eyes screwed in concentration as we ordered drinks and starters. He wrote down our orders and looked up.

"I love the accent. Where are you guys from?"

"Britain."

"Well bless your heart. That's so cool. What language do they speak there?"

BAR–NAR–NAR

Everybody woke early with the thrill of excitement at spending our first day as residents of a new country together. We clearly needed a few things like coats and jumpers. With the Siberian weather conditions showing no signs of abating, there was no way we could wait for the boat to arrive with all of our goods, it would take months. So, after quickly walking Bandit and Scout around the apartment blocks to find a patch of grass to pee on, we all jumped in the car and headed off to North Point Mall.

The mall was pretty quiet as it was a weekday and most people were back in work and school. First off, we needed jumpers, so we braved the 'Fierce' aftershave-laden miasma of Abercrombie & Fitch. With music blaring and young, attractive shop assistants following me around, I found a zip-up jumper/jacket, thick and woolly enough to scale Everest in. It cost me the GDP of a small African country but was so heavily infused with that peculiar scent of Abercrombie that I have never needed to buy aftershave since.

Next up we needed a birthday present for Ben. His birthday is on the 28th of December and with the move imminent, we hadn't wanted to buy him something bulky that we would then have to struggle to move across to the USA. The other reason was that we were still in bribe mode, making sure that the kids were as bought into this move as much as possible and we intended to buy him a PlayStation. It made sense to buy one when we had arrived to get the right power cords and save on shipping.

Wandering aimlessly around the vastness that was Sears, I found a woolen scarf I liked. It was only $9.99 and I had a $10 note in my wallet, so I pulled it out and went up to the counter. The cheery sales lady smiled broadly as I handed her the scarf. She rang it up.

"That's just ten dollars and seventy-six cents."

"Excuse me?"

"That's just ten dollars and seventy-six cents," she repeated.

"But the price tag says nine dollars and ninety-nine."

The smile slipped away from her face as she realized she was dealing with not only an idiot, but from the accent, a foreign one at that.

"Yes. And with *tax*," she said slowly so that even I had a chance to understand, "that would be ten dollars and seventy-six cents."

Shit, I thought to myself. *Bloody, bastarding sales tax.* In the United Kingdom and all of Europe and indeed, many other countries around the world, sales tax, or VAT are always included in the sticker/tag price.

"Oh yeah, of course. Sorry," I muttered, reaching into my pocket for change. I pulled out an array of small coins and looked at them in quiet despair. I slowly came to the realization that the small assemblage of silver and copper shrapnel, that I had accumulated across various financial transactions, meant absolutely nothing to me. I recognized the dollar coin, but the rest all seemed to be about the same size with little to differentiate them.

I looked into the sales lady's icy glare and back at the coins. With no option left open to me, like a frail little old man, I held out my palm to her where the coins lay in a little pile.

I heard a distinct and barely concealed tut and my now openly hostile sales lady took the appropriate change from my palm, handed me my bagged scarf and receipt, and turned her back on me.

We were all getting hungry so we popped across the road from the mall to a Ruth's Chris Steak House. We had never been to one before so we were not prepared for how wildly wallet-emptying such an experience could turn out to be. Ben's eyes lit up as he perused all of the steak options, but Adam's brow was furrowed in concern. Ben will eat anything but prefers menu items that are on the breathtakingly pricey side. Adam was (and still is) a picky eater. He *will* eat meat, but only if all resemblance to the animal has been removed, it has been carved into the shape of a dinosaur and then coated in breadcrumbs.

To minimize the damage to my wallet I ordered for Ben and then the waiter turned to ask Adam what he would like.

"I'll take the French fries please," he answered.

"Of course. And that comes with three sides."

"Hmmm. I'll take the mash...the baked potato...and the waffle fries."

"Ahh, yes, potato four ways, an excellent choice," said the waiter with a barely concealed smirk.

The same waiter managed to really anger Ben later after the steaks and mounds of endless potato dishes had been consumed.

"What would you like for dessert?" he asked Ben.

"I would like the banana split please."

The waiter let out an uncontrolled bark of laughter, quickly stifled behind a hand raised quickly to his mouth, and we could all hear him muttering to himself, shoulders shaking with laughter as he walked away, "bar-nar-nar. bar-nar-nar."

After lunch I dropped Paula and the boys back at the apartment as, in the afternoon, I had a meeting with Carel in the office to pretend that I had not come here solely for a prolonged American vacation, but instead to actually do some work for him.

Dressed in shirt and trousers I drove to the office and dropped my laptop off with IT so that they could load and configure whatever they needed to allow me access to the US data networks. Carel had booked a meeting room. We shook hands and I thanked him, very sincerely, for the opportunity.

"So, did you figure out which accounts I am getting? I hear that we have Bank of America, UPS, and Verizon Wireless all here in Atlanta. It would be amazing to work on those."

"Yeah, but I got Doug to pick those accounts up."

"Doug from Texas?"

"Yup."

"OK, great, I guess, so what do I get?"

"Well to start with, you will have Toronto Dominion, Bell Canada, Rogers, and The Hartford."

"But those are all either North-west accounts or, unless the name deceives me, accounts in Canada."

"Yeah."

"But I just moved to Atlanta..."

"Yeah, I know but I think these will be a good fit for you. They are all big technical accounts with big problems."

"Sounds great," I said sarcastically, which was obviously lost on Carel, "and the Hartford."

"Yep."

"*The* Hartford."

"Yeah," this time almost with an apology in his voice.

The Hartford had been one of our company's first and largest customers. Even in the UK, four-thousand miles away they were nothing if not notorious for being our biggest 'pain in the ass' customer. It sounded like a stitch-up to me, but I was largely unfazed. I had two big things going for me, I had a winning smile and the sweetest of English accents.

LIBERTY

We had the rental car free for the first three months but we were keen to get our own car picked out and ordered. The last car I had bought in the UK had taken close to twelve weeks from selection and deposit in the showroom to its actual arrival at the dealership. A Subaru I had bought previously had taken closer to six months before I could pick it up and drive it home, so we wanted to at least get the ball rolling and get one ordered. Who knew how long it might take to buy a car in America.

Paula quite fancied a Jeep Liberty so we set off to the Alpharetta Highway, close to where we had sat in the Humvee six or seven months prior. The sales guy came out, all smiles and handshakes, as we looked around the lot. His name was Brand and he asked us the usual questions, expecting us to be the usual tire kickers, but when we told him we wanted to buy a car he got right down to business. Brand told us he loved our accents and asked us if we knew somebody called John who he thought might live in London. We told him that we did indeed know somebody called John who lived in London, although we admitted the smallest possibility that it may not be the same one that he knew, and also that we would like to test drive a Liberty.

Brand looked at us a little nervously when we presented him with our tatty old paper UK driving licenses, but he photocopied them, accepting that they were valid purely on face value, and asked us which Liberty we would like to take out. Out in the lot was a row of brand-new cars, white silver, red and blue; Paula particularly liked the bright red one. Brand disappeared for a few minutes and came back with the key and ten minutes later I was pulling off the lot into four lanes of light traffic to take the test drive in the bright winter sunshine. We drove up the hill past the other dealerships, past Taquerias, nail salons, and fast-food outlets. In the distance, bright against the blue of the sky snapped the largest American flag I had ever seen, a vast emblem of wealth and prosperity. A fluttering red, white and blue, star-spangled homage to capitalism.

Back at the dealership, we told Brand that we would love to buy a Jeep Liberty from him. He asked us if we liked the red one and we told him we did, a red one would be perfect. He disappeared into the back for a few minutes and came back with a small novel of paperwork which we slowly and diligently filled out. With that complete, he disappeared once more and when he came back, he plonked a car key in front of us and told us he would be right back.

Paula and I sat blinking at each other in silence for a few minutes.

"Did we just buy a car?" I asked her.

"I don't really know," she said.

"I think we did. I think that, maybe, that red Liberty we just test-drove is now ours."

"Nooo...surely not?"

"You ask him when he comes back."

"Why me?"

"Because I'm the guy and I'm supposed to know things about cars."

Brand returned and Paula asked him, somewhat nervously, if we had just bought the red Liberty. Now it was Brand's turn to look nervous.

"You...sure...did. Is that OK?"

Paula and I exchanged glances. Nothing worked this quickly in the UK. Not for a new car, a second-hand one on a used lot sure, but nowhere in the UK could you walk into a dealership and drive away in a brand-new car, that's just not how things worked.

"Of course, it's ok, but I'm just not sure how you would like us to pay for it?'

"Oh, a personal check is just fine."

All I had was my temporary checks from Bank of America. I had moved a bunch of money across from the house sale in the UK, so we did have sufficient funds in the bank to pay for the car, but once again we found ourselves completely out of our depth. Nobody pays for a car in the UK with a check, in that nobody, individual or business, anywhere, would *accept* a personal check for anywhere close to the thirty-thousand dollars that was the asking price for this car.

"Are you sure a check will be OK?" I asked.

Now, Brand looked really worried, and his eyes narrowed in suspicion that we were somehow not the charming English couple we appeared to be, but fraudsters about to steal one of his cars and head for the border.

"Yep. Well, we know where you live," he laughed nervously, "that is, if you put your correct addresses on the forms."

We assured him we did; I checked the total on the sales invoice and wrote a check, noting to myself that once more I had forgotten to add sales tax to the total. My mental calculations were out by over two thousand dollars this time. I really needed to get much better at this.

Twenty minutes later we had the Liberty parked outside of the apartments, laughing at how stupid we both felt, but happy that one more hurdle was out of the way. We had overcome it together. Now we just needed to get our driving licenses sorted.

A Test

We had both diligently ignored the whole American driving license issue. It had been the great big grey thing with a trunk and big ears seated across from us in the living room ever since we had arrived. You can't, technically at least, take your test in a rental car, although in truth nobody at the Georgia DMV will check. But, by law, you are supposed to get a Georgia driving license within thirty days of taking up residence in the state and it was long past time to knuckle down and get it done.

I found a testing center in Norcross and we both started swotting up on the driving handbook that we had downloaded from the Department of Driving Services, the equivalent to the UK's highway code.

The rules for driving a car, of course, are broadly the same. The most important distinction to observe is that in the USA we drive on the right and in the UK, we drive on the left. The other obvious distinction was that before you even get to the first page of the DDS booklet, it has a full page dealing with what to do *when* you are pulled over by the police and offers such sterling advice such as:

'Keep your hands on the wheel at all times so they are clearly observable.'

'Let the officer know if you have a weapon in the vehicle.'

'Wait for the officer's instructions before reaching for your driver's license.'

These are three phrases you will not see in the British highway code which deals much more with the safe passing of horses, and giving way to vicars on bicycles when encountered unexpectedly down narrow country lanes.

Back when we studied for our license exam there were no limits on cellphone use when driving. In fact, it seemed to be mandatory for at least one hand to be occupied in an activity unrelated to driving at all times. We were shocked one morning when all of us were together in the car, when I was forced to brake hard to pull up to the end of a line of traffic on GA400. We had been driving at over 70mph, so we were all surprised to see the lady driver in the car next to us, windows down, eating cornflakes out of a cereal box she had filled with milk. The car was covered in 'Jesus saves' stickers and the little Samaritan fish emblem. She held the cereal box in her left hand and a spoon dripping with breakfast in the other. She looked at us all staring at her, all of our mouths agape for a second, and then the electric blackout windows on her car rose to conceal her. How she pressed the window raise button or indeed drive was a mystery. She must have been steering the car with her knees, or perhaps, that morning, Jesus had indeed been at the wheel.

Based on the standard of the driving we had experienced so far in Atlanta, it had to be said that the actual driving test was something we weren't too worried about. It was the theory exam that was going to be a challenge.

We studied and studied and tested each other until we believed we were as proficient as we were ever going to become. I booked the tests back-to-back, one for me and one for Paula, in Norcross for a few days hence, and then we waited for the fateful morning in trepidation.

Me and Ben have always had a somewhat cavalier attitude to passing tests. We both figure out what the minimum passing percentage is and then aim for precisely one more percentage point than that so that we allow for a suitably safe buffer. Paula and Adam tend to stress about exam situations. They learn the material as well, or better than me and Ben, but then turn into wobbly mind-blanked zombies the instant somebody starts the countdown timer.

The fateful morning came clear and blue as usual, and with it our hearts sank and the butterflies began to flutter. I drove us to Norcross and we parked up the Liberty, and with sweaty palms, we walked into the busy testing center. We took tickets and sat waiting for a few minutes until our numbers were called almost together.

We did the eye test first which involved looking through some sort of table-mounted binocular device and reading out to the examiner the large letter and number combination displayed therein. I have to say, if anybody failed this part of the test, they probably shouldn't have been allowed to walk unaided to the testing center without the support of a Labrador.

For the next part, we were led to a row of old computers and walked through the instructions. In Georgia at least, there are a total of forty questions to be answered. There are twenty questions on road signs, fifteen of which you must answer correctly, and another twenty on road safety, again, fifteen of which must be correctly answered in order to proceed to the actual driving test. So, a 75% pass rate. I had my goal — 76%.

I began mine and cracked off a few of the initial questions. Some were blindingly obvious but some were more than open to interpretation. I glanced across at Paula who was busy, brow furrowed, hunched over her terminal. I couldn't tell if it was going well or not over there. The test only took ten minutes or so and I hit the finish button and received my score — 78%. Nobody likes an over-achiever.

I took a seat and waited for my number to be called again so that I could go and do the last stage of the process. As I waited, I saw Paula finish her computer test and walk out of the testing area. She looked both angry and upset. "Ruh-Roh Raggy" I muttered to myself. She had failed.

My number was called and while I tried to console Paula, my examiner approached me to take me outside. He was a white guy, just a bit younger than me. We sat in the Liberty and went through the procedures. I hit a cone on the reverse parking test but he didn't seem to notice or care. He directed me out of the parking lot, we took four right turns as we chatted about life in England. He knew somebody called John who lived in London and he wondered if I knew him, and then we ended up back in the testing center parking lot. The entire test had lasted five minutes and we had essentially just driven around the block. I had passed. It was, thankfully, ridiculously easy.

A week later, back at the same testing center, Paula passed her test. She handed in her ragged, torn paper UK driving license and we took home our shiny plastic USA driving licenses, both happy that this stressful step was over and done with.

School Time

It was finally time for the extended vacation to come to an end. We had been here almost a month and work beckoned me; I had my first meeting scheduled in a couple of days. I was required to fly out to present our software architecture to a team of techies in Washington D.C. It all sounded so much cooler to me somehow than driving to Wolverhampton to do, essentially, the same thing.

The Bank of America bank cards had arrived so we knew the postal address worked. Still no sign of the social security cards, but that was to be expected. It was time for me to start work and it was also time to get the kids off the PlayStation and into the USA school system.

We had been told by Wendi that the best schools were Crabapple Middle School and Roswell High School. The age of the boys meant they would both have to start in middle school even though Ben would only be there for one semester.

We drove to Crabapple Middle School as a family to meet with the headteacher. By signing the kids into this school district, it also meant that ultimately, we were committing ourselves to living within the same catchment area. The headteacher was sweet enough, she was interested in Ben more than Adam as he had impressive school records from his English high school, especially in regard to mathematics. They were accepted easily enough but, despite bringing all of their vaccination certificates, the school required us to have them all done afresh.

Now we were solidly into the whole really living in America vibe. Schools and injections. What could be more real life than that, nothing like a dash of misery and pain to really bring it home. With injections done and documented on the correct forms that the US educational system would accept, the kids were due in school on Monday.

Meanwhile, I had my meeting in Washington to attend to. I had spoken with the salesman, a guy called Dan, and we had arranged to meet at the departure gate in Hartsfield Jackson. This would be a day trip. Fly to Washington, attend the all-day architecture workshop, and then fly back to ATL later that afternoon. I got up at six in the morning and showered as quietly as I could in the En-suite. I jumped in the car and drove to the airport. It was my first experience of commuter traffic in Atlanta and it was awful. I thought I was going to miss my flight just getting onto the highway. I parked up, cleared security, and bought a bottle of Coca-Cola from the shop at the top of the escalator. The large black lady behind the counter of the shop greeted me with a smile.

"God bless you sir, how's your day going?"

"Very well thank you. And yours?"

"Jesus *himself* is smiling down on me right now, thank you for asking."

I am *very* far from religious but she was a delight and I smiled broadly as I handed her the money for the Coke, "thanks. Bye."

"Now you just have yourself a blessed and Jesus-filled day honey."

I would get to know this lady well and she was always the same, every morning, rain or shine, no matter how ridiculously early or late it was, whenever I flew through ATL we would exchange pleasantries as I bought my Coca-Cola, and she would bestow some baby Jesus based blessing upon me, which I always accepted in the good spirit it was given.

With Coke in hand, I met Dan at the departure gate. We boarded and joined the long queue of planes taxiing out to one of ATL's five runways.

In the air, I sat looking out of the window as we approached Washington. I was hoping for views of the State Capitol building, the Washington Monument, and maybe even the White House. Of course, it was foggy and I didn't even see the ground until the wheels almost touched the ground. I was further disappointed when the taxi we took basically drove us out of the airport and turned left into an industrial park and dropped us off at an inauspicious-looking grey concrete tower block.

The organizer of the meeting met us at the security desk at reception. There were a few people already checking in for the meeting ahead of us. When we got our turn, it was obvious that the host knew Dan, he shook his hand and turned to me to say Hi and ask me my name.

"Andy."

He looked at me blankly, "come again?"

"Andy."

"Nope. One more time?"

For fucks sake, I thought, how hard can this be. It's only four bloody letters. I heard somebody in line before us introduce himself as Wojciech Wisniewska without anybody batting an eye, but here I was struggling with getting the concept of A-N-D-Y across.

"Andy," I almost shouted.

"Randy?"

"No. Andy."

What was wrong with this guy?

"Mohammad?"

"No!"

Dan jumped in for me, aware of my rising frustration, "his name is Andy."

What was interesting was the pronunciation, and I took note. In the UK, especially in the north of England, the leading "A" in Andy is pronounced very flat as in "<u>a</u>sk." The way Dan pronounced it, it sounded more like the first vowel sound in "<u>e</u>rr."

Finally, with our names, thankfully, on little stickers on our jackets, we joined the others in the boardroom. The meeting went on for hour after hour, with each company in attendance presenting their solution for a period of thirty or forty minutes. There were about fifty people in attendance in total. It was two in the afternoon when my turn came. I set up my slides and turned to the whiteboard to sketch out a sample architecture of how our software connected. As I sketched, I talked, animated, and at my usual talking pace. The room was very quiet so, after only a minute or two, I turned around to see every face in the audience staring at me open-mouthed, not having understood a single word that I had said.

"Sorry," I said, "I just got here from England. Let me start again, only this time I will speak *much* slower."

In the end, the meeting was a success, but I learned some valuable lessons. I had brought with me an accent that was apparently almost indecipherable to most Americans and coupled with that, I spoke way too quickly. And, of course, my name from that moment forward was "Erndy."

On my flight back home, I received one of those emails that make you feel a bit sick. After all of the planning and meetings to get our visa organized with the company, Nick, my old CEO, the one who had advocated for me to come over here, had sent a companywide message telling us that he had just sold the company and that on Monday, we would all be working for a different company. I had no idea where that left me, where we stood with the validity of the visa, or even with the job, on the basis of which I had just moved my entire life and family across the Atlantic for.

Back home, we enjoyed the weekend together and then on Monday morning, we drove the kids to their new school to begin their first day, following the long line of yellow buses into the circle. We dropped the kids off at the entrance and then I had to drop Paula off back at the apartment so that I could head into the office. I had some urgent calls to make.

I spoke to Carel and he was all full of calm and reassurance. He didn't foresee any changes to his team or my employment. But I was highly aware that my visa was tied to the job. If I lost my job, the visa was rendered invalid. We would then have thirty days in which to vacate the country. Our furniture hadn't even arrived yet, worse case, we might all have been deported before it even got here.

I was a tad nervous as you can imagine, and it was the primary reason that I requested that we should begin the green card process immediately. The green card would provide Paula and I with the independence to seek work elsewhere in the USA should the new owners of the company decide to start cutting expensive positions. Especially ones brand new to the organization. Carel agreed to look into it with Human Resources and I drove to pick up Paula to go and get the kids from their first day at school.

As we pulled up, back in line behind the school buses at Crabapple Middle School, I admit to being terribly nervous. What if the boys hated it? What if they came out in tears? We scanned the hundreds of faces that poured out of the exit doors and then we saw Ben. He was surrounded by a bunch of tall, black girls, all giggling at his cute accent. He was the color of a Tom-ar-Toe, and grinning from ear to ear.

In the middle of all of this, I had to leave town for a week to attend the company's annual 'Sales Kickoff' in Phoenix. The sales kickoff is an excuse to get all of the sales teams together, at incredible expense, to bore the shit out of them with endless PowerPoints delivered in windowless, airless rooms, to people so wretchedly hungover that they could barely speak, never mind ingest the cunning new selling strategies that the company was pretending it had come up with.

I hated every single event. It was always the worst week of my year. My favorite week of the year was the week after I returned home from sales kickoff, and then the weeks got gradually worse until the next one finally came around. Unfortunately, it meant that I would have to leave Paula, to drop off and pick up the kids and get around town to do the grocery shopping and all of the other day-to-day minutia, all on her own.

I called her up midweek to see how she was coping with all of the three-lane roads and manic traffic. She wasn't happy. In the morning she had taken the kids to the cinema, planning on taking the back roads as it was only a couple of miles away. Unfortunately, we still didn't know our way around so, like me, she was using sat nav to get everywhere. The Tom Tom decided the interstate would save twenty seconds or so, and subsequently directed her onto the slip road to join GA400 in the rush hour. Before she realized it, it was too late, and she was forced to join the interstate, her first time. She was in bits, scared, and really upset.

Ben had shouted words of encouragement as she merged into the fast-moving mayhem and Adam had rubbed her shoulders from the back seat to soothe her shredded nerves until she managed to pull off at the very next exit.

House Hunting

Time was flying and we were coming up to the end of the first month in our rented apartment. We needed to start looking for a permanent house. Paula started to work her magic, figuring out a list of all of the things we wanted in a house and all of the things we needed to avoid.

We called up Wendi who, surprisingly, was still willing to work with us and we set up some viewings. There was almost nothing on the market with a swimming pool and this was a promise I had made to Paula. If we moved to a hot country, part of the deal, non-negotiable, was a swimming pool. What nobody told us was that the housing market in Atlanta is incredibly seasonal. We were looking in January and this is well known (not to us obviously), to be the time that almost nobody buys and nobody sells. The time to buy and sell in Atlanta is spring through summer. What we learned much later is that Atlanta, like many other large cities in the USA, is an itinerant city, not many people who live there were actually born in Georgia. Companies bring employees in and move them out to other postings, in other cities when the schools are closed, and that was months away.

Without this knowledge, we were severely handicapped. We felt like the three-month lease was forcing our hand. What we should have done, if anybody had chosen to share true market conditions with us, was to have simply rented the apartment ourselves for another three months or more. That would have put us dead center into moving season.

It is good advice we have offered to other friends who moved out to the United States. Take your time. Rent for a good while, and get a better feeling for all of the possible neighborhoods. Do speak to more than one realtor, many have a favorite area they prefer to do business in, which will skew your options; don't be rushed into a bad decision.

We looked at houses in Roswell, Alpharetta, and as far out as Woodstock and even Canton. Some were brick construction; many were timber framed with either siding which was fine, or stucco which nobody in the realtor business seemed to care for. We knew we wanted a house with a pool on an absolutely level, turfed, and landscaped lot with a large patio on the outside, but not so much land that it would be hard to care for. The house needed to be a relatively recent build, nothing too old, three to four bedrooms with a large picture window in the main living room to let in lots of light. If the house had a basement, it needed to be finished and modern.

So of course, we almost immediately made an offer on a huge and aging four-bedroom house, with a dingy and insect-ridden, partly finished basement. The house had small pokey windows in every room and dark wood paneling on the walls that seemed to absorb the few photons that made it through. It was balanced on the crown of a precipitously steep quarter-acre hill, all of which was covered in towering pine trees, kudzu, and a rampant ivy that strangled all other growth. There wasn't a patch of grass to be seen and, of course, no pool.

We now had an experience similar to our car-buying episode. Buying a house in the USA is very different from doing the same in the UK. In England, a house can sit on the market for months, years sometimes. When somebody does finally make an offer there is no commitment on either side to actually proceed with the sale. No contracts, no earnest money down, and no dates to close agreed upon; either party can simply walk away at any point, including the day before actual contracts are due to exchange. In the USA, we found it all a little different. We signed a contract, put earnest money down, and agreed to a thirty-day close. It was all shockingly efficient.

Thirty days went by surprisingly quickly. Luckily, we didn't have anything to move other than ourselves, the dogs, the paranoid cat, and our cases.

The day of the closing dawned bright and cold. We dropped the boys off at school and then drove to the closing attorney's building in Sandy Springs. We parked the car and were ushered into a modern and sterile boardroom. We met our sellers for the first time, a nice older couple who were moving to Florida. We were all seated and the attorney began sending pieces of paper around the table in a clockwise direction from the large pile in front of him. Each form was explained, although much of the American verbiage was beyond me, but it was made very clear that if you didn't sign, the house sale wouldn't go through. So, we all signed it and passed it on to the next person to our left. My signature got gradually worse as the procession of forms continued until even I wouldn't have recognized it, and then, ten minutes later, with wrists aching and fingers cramping we were done. The ziplock bag with the house keys and garage door openers was pushed across the table. I took out my checkbook and suddenly had a blinding headache. I had never written a number this big in my life, and my hand shook.

I laughingly explained the sudden tremor to the attorney.

"Well, bless your heart."

There was that charming Georgia phrase again. People were so nice here. I managed to shakingly scrawl the large number, date it, and produce another poor effigy of my signature on the check. I handed it to the attorney. The house was ours.

We drove to the house and used the garage door opener to get inside. It was the strangest feeling. We felt like housebreakers intruding upon somebody else's property. And yet, here we were. In just a little over a month we had bought a house in America. We spent the rest of the day driving backwards and forwards, between the apartment and the house, moving cases filled with clothes and other belongings. And last of all two worried dogs who looked at us with eyes filled with suspicion, and one terrified cat.

We had no furniture so we drove to Best Buy and bought the biggest TV we could fit into the car. Then onto Walmart to buy some inflatable beds. We borrowed some pillows and bedsheets from the apartment. We set the TV up in the corner of the living room and used the box it came in as a table. At three in the afternoon, we picked up the kids from school and bought pizza on the way home to settle in for the first night in our new home.

We didn't have cable yet so we set up the PlayStation and sat as a family, cross-legged on the floor playing Spiro the Dragon and Crash Bandicoot. As night fell the warm and comfortable house suddenly became dark and oppressive. Looking out of the uncovered windows, all we could see was a total inky blackness and our own reflections looking back at us. It gave the impression that hidden things were out there, in the woods, looking back at us. We picked out by the brightness, they, lurking in the darkness with nefarious intent.

After dinner, me and Adam took the dogs out for a last walk around the neighborhood. It was dark and cold so we walked fast. The neighborhood was old and composed mainly of big wood-framed houses set far back from the road. Most lots were filled with trees and only a few windows held a welcoming light. We got to the end of the road and froze when we saw a shape slip from behind one of the houses. The light from the streetlight picked out the two yellow gleams of its eyes as it looked back at us. It moved quickly, low to the ground and we didn't wait to see if it was a rabid coyote or a harmless possum. We scuttled back around the corner and up our ridiculously steep drive to seek safety.

When we got home the house was in a furor. Seated on the floor, Paula had been more than startled to find small scorpions creeping from under the door that led down into our basement. It was one of those basements that you only find in movies like The Evil Dead and the Amityville Horror and, for as long as we lived there, I was terrified of it and spent as little time down there, cleaning furnace filters or whatever, as I absolutely had to.

I was sent to explore the source of this scorpion invasion and found that they were coming in through a room at the front of the house that had been sold to us as a 'wine cellar' but on closer inspection, more closely resembled the hole in the ground where Buffalo Bill starved his victims to better make a suit out of female human skins.

We started to wonder not only why we had bought this huge and scary house, but also why we had moved to such a wild and inhospitable land.

In the morning I called up the Gas, Electricity, and Comcast cable TV companies to get the utilities transferred into our name. But of course, each time we got to the bit where the agents asked for our social security number, we were turned down because we still didn't have it yet. The only way to get the utilities into our name was to drive across the railroad tracks to the dodgy side of town, find the local offices, and queue along with all of the other poor folks to write deposit checks.

I also called up the pest control company whose services we had secured for a period of twelve months with the purchase of this house, only to be told that, for some reason, they declined to explain, they didn't do scorpions. I could only assume they were as frightened of them as we were.

A New Best Friend

Slowly, piece by piece and bit by bit we settled in. We put up blinds and curtains and bought more lamps to banish the darkness and we explored the neighborhood. We were invited to a Superbowl party and met some of the neighbors. We immediately liked Dominic and Maria and we were immediately scared by Mark who had a face more intense than Jack Nicholson in The Shining and who possessed twelve guns, one for each one of his fingers. He was married to Jenny, a woman so perpetually drunk that all of the other neighbors, who had tired of cleaning carpets from spilled drinks, had all chipped in to buy her a sippy cup from which she glugged either red wine, Jägermeister, or tequila depending on whether it was breakfast, lunch or dinner.

I bought some insect control chemicals and a sprayer and took care of the scorpions myself. I also started spraying for cockroaches, of which there was a seemingly unstoppable amount. These were American cockroaches and we were all terrified and freaked out by them in equal amounts. We hadn't seen anything like them. Up to two inches long and faster than Usain Bolt, they made us jump and squeal whenever we happened upon them, which was often.

In bed one night, just about to go to sleep, I saw one creep out of the sunken spotlights above our bed. It dropped heavily onto our bed covers. I told Paula to stay still, not to move a muscle, so that we didn't spark it into scurrying for cover, only to realize I was now in bed alone and talking to myself. I threw back the bedsheets with a squeal and it ran around in a frenetic little circle and then just disappeared. We pulled the covers and stripped the bed but it was nowhere to be found. It was clearly still on, in, or under the bed, we just couldn't find it. Another sleepless night just waiting for the monster to crawl into an ear or other vulnerable orifice. I figured that the attic, possibly an even scarier place than the basement, might be the place they were coming from.

The next day I gave myself a manly talking to, filled my spray cannister, and mounted the drop-down attic steps. I had a flashlight in one hand and peered into the beam-crossed, spiderweb-strewn darkness. The boiler kicked into life just as I took my first hesitant step onto the rafters, making me jump. I started to spray the rafters, joists, and insulating material as I carefully navigated my way across the dusty space, balancing on the beams above the fragile plaster ceiling. Suddenly, as I sprayed, the floor of the attic came to scuttling life at my feet. Cockroaches. Swift and scuttling, writhing, rustling, they fled, panicked before me, swarming over each other, away from and towards me.

There were thousands of them and it took all of my nerve not to just step through the ceiling and plunge to the floor below to escape them. I sprayed and hopped from cringing foot to cringing foot and sprayed and screamed silently, backing up to the steps to climb down panting and brushing invisible bugs from my skin and clothing. It did work though. We still saw the occasional one here or there but we were slowly gaining control and getting used to them (a bit).

We began to realize that this was just another generous gift of the Deep South. Mosquitos, cockroaches, and termites were a part of life here. You could fight them and try and control them but they encroached on any part of the house not constantly protected.

We finally had some good news on the storage container. It was due at the end of the week, this now being the very end of February. We had some furniture at this point. Paula and I had gone crazy in a furniture store in Roswell and bought the largest pieces of furniture you have ever seen. I had a desk and matching office chair that John D. Rockefeller would have been proud of. My USA geography was appalling, so on the wall behind my desk, I had purchased and pinned up a huge map of the United States. Paula had stuck a bright orange arrow to the map. She had written "you are here," on it and aimed its point towards Atlanta. Whenever Carel or one of the sales guys called to ask me to attend a meeting I would find a way to delay while I dragged my finger around the map muttering to myself, "Des Moines, Des Moines, come on where are you...?"

We also bought a Cal King bed so high and a mattress so lofty we really needed the ladder I had left behind in England in order to climb onto it.

One cold bright morning in early March a huge removal truck with the symbol of a giant peach backed slowly up our hill, and what seemed to be the entire population of Mexico sprang into action. Less than two hours later, all of our meager belongings were installed in the appropriate rooms.

That night we sat on our own British leather recliner watching our gigantic American TV, sipping tea out of our own British mugs, trying to choose from the 300 channels of utter shite that our expensive cable subscription had beamed into our room.

Despite being surrounded by all of our belongings we didn't sleep well that night. In the morning we were driving north, to Canton, to choose a Labrador puppy from a breeder that Paula had found on the internet. Paula was struggling to settle into our new American life. The house we had picked out was too large but also too isolated. In the UK, we were used to seeing people, neighbors, and friends. Back in the UK we walked everywhere, walked the kids to school, walked to the shops, walked to the pub. Here in the USA, we were forced to drive *everywhere*. The kids got picked up by the big yellow bus in the morning and dropped off again in the afternoon.

I was busy working, and flying in and out of Toronto and Connecticut. When Paula did leave the house, she shopped all alone and then, returning home, she drove back up our steep hill and parked the car in the garage. Paula missed her three sisters and found the USA to be isolating and strange. It was hard to make friends here. We all spoke the same language but culturally we were worlds apart and the gap seemed impossible to bridge. She did love dogs though and we thought the challenge of a puppy would consume much of her spare time and might help her adjust.

In the morning we woke early and we all jumped in the Liberty and drove on unfamiliar roads to Canton. We parked up on the road outside a ranch house that stood on a large, hilly pine-covered lot. The foothills of the Appalachians were already making their lofty presence known this far north.

There was a total of seven puppies in the litter, all yellow Labs. We had expected small mewling puppies, freshly separated from mom, but these were a few months old, round, and rumbustious with big floppy limbs and folds of flesh under glossy coats. They bounded around the pen the breeder had set up. One girl sat quietly in the corner and Paula was drawn to that one, but I liked another that bounced and sprang, a jumble of big paws and flapping ears. She had startlingly green eyes, a beauty spot on a pink nose, and lighter yellow markings across her shoulders that resembled Angel wings. We named her Tybee after the island close to Savannah where we had vacationed. She is the same beautiful girl you can see on the cover of this book you are holding.

I drove home, Paula seated next to me with Tybee sitting heavily on her knee, panting in the warm air from the open window. She made herself right at home and became an instant and adored member of the family. She would greet the boys home from school, bounding in great leaps through the trees, and down the hill to knock them off their feet. We walked her for miles in the Leita Thompson Park, just across the road from our neighborhood. Her eyes slowly faded from green to yellow but she never lost her angel wings. Paula took her to puppy training classes and ran the trails with her. She was a delight.

A Truck, A Pool and A Possum

We had been forced by our own circumstances to be cash buyers for a few months now, still struggling with having no credit rating or standing with any financial institutions. Luckily, due to a clerical error, the company I worked for had been paying me my American salary in British Pounds. It meant that I had to convert them to USD and eat the transaction fees. What worked was that the exchange rate was massively in our favor. Of course, it didn't last; they unfortunately soon realized their error. But during that sweet time, Paula had convinced herself that everything thing in America was close to half price and did all of her purchasing calculations in British pounds.

But it was tough not having any credit rating and it complicated every transaction and interaction, and then out of the blue, our social security cards arrived in the mail. Almost simultaneously, our mailbox was overwhelmed with offers of credit, credit cards, mortgages, and loans. Our American Amex cards arrived shortly after and all of our challenges with bigger purchases just went away.

One morning we went to our local branch of Bank of America. We wanted to exchange about fifty pounds of British currency we had left in wallets and jean pockets and get good ole US dollars back in return. The cash we had was all in notes, a few tens, a twenty, and a fiver or two. In Europe, you could take *any* currency into *any* bank and exchange it for the local currency. This was a large branch of Bank of America in a large town, but when presented with the request and the crumpled bills they all looked at us like we were Bonnie and Clyde trying to pull an international money heist.

The teller called her manager and then the manager called the branch manager. They all huddled in the back whispering. It was clear that this was the first time they had ever been asked to action such a strange ask. Some significant amount of time passed and phone calls to head office were made. Then one of them seemed to recall something she had been told on a training course at the very beginning of her long career. She disappeared into the back office and returned with a piece of dusty cardboard, maybe three feet in length and two feet tall. It was dog-eared and yellowed by the sun and years of neglect. It had perhaps, been used to prop open a door or something similar. On it were printed pictures of all of the banknotes of the United Kingdom with notes typed below.

The teller picked up each one of our notes and carefully compared it to the pictures, nodding her head wisely as each one magically matched its pictured counterpart. About an hour and a half later we finally left with our UK cash exchanged for dollar bills. We thanked the teller and the manager and we got the standard response.

"Well now, bless your heart."

Everybody was just *so* nice.

We had managed for several weeks now with just the one car. But it meant that whenever I needed to head to the airport and travel, sometimes for a few days, Paula was stranded in the house, or I was reliant on taxis, which were rare and wildly expensive in Atlanta in the years before Uber appeared on the scene. I needed a car of my own.

I found what I needed at the local CarMax on the Alpharetta Highway in Roswell. I picked out a secondhand bright blue Dodge Ram 1500 5.9-liter V8 twin cab truck for only $8000. It looked just like the one I had mocked as being far too large and much too obscene on our first visit together a year before. And now here I was, only a few months later, driving my big ass pickup, burbling down the Alpharetta highway, one hand on the steering wheel, coffee in the other with my American Labrador by my side, sun in my eyes, living my best American life.

I did begin to question my choice the following day as I had to fly out of ATL once more, to attend a very shouty meeting in Toronto. I drove to the airport thinking of parking in what I had come to think of as my own personal parking space, on the top level of the long-stay parking lot at South Terminal. It was always fairly busy, but I normally flew out on a Monday and would come back mid-week or later. This time I was flying out on a Wednesday and all of the on-site parking lots were full. I was forced to leave the airport and find one of the offsite parking lots that are sprinkled around College Park.

I found a Wally Park and drove the truck around the busy lot looking for an empty space. Most places like this in America, have sensibly adopted the angled parking bays that Europe refuses to embrace.

Angled bays are easy to drive into and reverse out of. Unfortunately, this particular Wally Park had decided to maximize profits over convenience. The only narrow space I could find was surrounded by other cars and the only way to get into it with my outsize truck was to reverse into it. I swallowed hard and then, as I started the maneuver, the worst thing possible happened. The shuttle bus, crowded with other Wally Park customers all heading to the terminal, pulled up alongside me. The driver of the bus could see that I was parking, so he waved to me to continue doing so, so that I could then jump onto his bus for the short ride back to the terminal.

Having only just got the truck and only driven it down fifty straight miles, and only ever in a forward direction, I was fairly certain that reverse parking it into this tiny space was going to be beyond me, so I waved to the driver using the universal hand signals for, "no I'm fine, you go past, I'll get the next one."

The driver just shook his head and waved for me to continue parking.

I tried to motion him to continue past once more but he held up a hand, no. He was going to wait for me. Balls. I took a deep breath and, conscious of all of the eyes on the bus staring in my direction, I started to back the long bed of the truck slowly into the tight space. My truck was very secondhand and didn't possess any modern backup camera trickery. As soon as I started backing up, the extreme height and length of the bed concealed any reference points and I was left blindly hoping that the car behind me wasn't going to get too crushed. I managed to squeeze most of the truck into some of the space and not having heard any thumps or sounds of tinkling glass, called it done. I put the truck in park and jumped down with my backpack. As I boarded the bus, I received a warm round of applause from the other passengers and took myself a small bow.

Tybee loved that truck; we would ride all over the place together. She would sit next to me, panting happily as we drove to Home Depot and put a hammer and a small box of nails in the otherwise empty bed. The most I ever hauled was a couple of bags of mulch and a rake. Paula hated it, it was way too big and drove like crap. There were some strange stains on the cloth seats that refused to be removed and it smelt like a Las Vegas strip club, but I loved it.

It was about this time that we thought life was going too well and that we should add some stress, financial instability, and woe to our new American lives. We commissioned a pool to be built in the backyard. We decided to dig it out on a raised piece of ground in the backyard. Paula found a Floridian guy called Jeff to build the pool and then the mayhem commenced.

We needed to take out a huge tree that grew pretty much in the location of where the deep end needed to be. Taking Jeff's advice, we called the city to get a permit. What we should have done was to drive to the 'Silver Skillet' diner on the corner of Roswell Road and Norcross and pick up five or six of the Mexicans with chainsaws, who were always there in the morning looking for work. But no, we engaged with the city, and time and money began to simply fritter and flutter away in the winds of bureaucracy. In the end, that tree and all of the permits added about $12,000 to the pool project.

The pool got dug, but then Jeff realized that the shallow end was too high. So, despite having just removed three hundred tons of soil to dig the hole for the pool, he now realized that he actually needed to bring in another three hundred tons of soil to shore up the far end, and then build a retaining wall to stop the entire thing from sliding back down the hill and into our neighbors yard.

We were super excited to see it finished though and filled it with water only to find that when we stepped inside for a paddle and a swim, the base, which should have been firm, was instead soft and we left footprints wherever we walked. We refused to settle the remainder of the bill. Eager to embrace all experiences that were American, we then had our first exciting brush with an American lawsuit. After several threatening letters in both directions, Jeff backed down and we put the money in the bank to repair the pool with another contractor at a future date.

Tybee was growing up but still kept the angel wing markings across her shoulders. One night she was out in the backyard for longer than was typical to have a last pee before we all turned in for bed. When I shouted at her, she came trotting in, all soft smiling eyes with something in her mouth. She deposited a large dirty-looking animal on our front room rug, in front of the TV, and stood back waiting for our thanks. It was the size of a large ugly cat with long whiskers. It had a greyish body and a pointed snout. A dead possum. We had never seen one before but we knew we wanted it out of the house tout de suite. I grabbed a dustpan and a large Tupperware bowl from the kitchen, the one Paula used for whisking cream and tossing salads, and scooped the thing onto the dustpan and placed the Tupperware over its body.

It was then that we found out why the phrase 'playing possum' was so well known. The 'dead' possum stopped playing possum and sprang back into lively and panicked possummy life. It scuttled around on my dustpan, thankfully trapped by the Tupperware. Holding the dustpan and creature at arm's length, I too panicked and ran for the kitchen door. I walked across the patio and, under cover of darkness, deposited the thing over the neighbor's fence.

As part of the pool permit, we had to build a fence, and it was a sizeable lot to fence in. We found two good old Georgia boys advertising their 'handyman' services in the local newspaper. They were called Ben and Randy and they started work straight away. They were both corn and steak-fed, 230 lbs. a piece, and strong as oxen. They both chewed 'tobaccy' which was new to us, we thought that was a thing constrained to movies about the American Civil War and the occasional episode of The Dukes of Hazard. They both always had one cheek loaded like a chipmunk and left little pools of brown and sticky spit all over the yard and the patio, which we had to shoo the dogs away from before they licked it up.

The other problem was that we couldn't understand a single word they said. They were the most, deep south folks, we had ever come across, and we were forced to communicate largely through hand gestures and drawing shapes into the Georgia clay with a stick. They did a really good job with the fence but the gate, and the arcane concept of hinges, were technically far beyond their pooled intellects. When they finished it, I went over to try it out. I unlatched the gate and pulled it open but it immediately hit the obstruction of the hill. With more hand gestures I motioned that the gate should have opened outward, away from the hill, but I just couldn't get them to understand, so I changed it over myself when they had finally been paid and left.

With the pool and the fence finally finished I busied myself with pool cleaning and balancing chemicals. Ask most people in the USA about pools and they will moan and complain that they are just too much trouble, too much work, too expensive. I loved my pool. I loved cleaning it and I loved playing with the chemicals. It was like one huge chemistry set, albeit one that occasionally reddened eyes and singed skin.

I had only had the pool operational for a couple of weeks when I went up the hill to clean the skimmers out. The skimmers are designed to allow the pumps to pull water through little baskets located under maintenance covers. They trap all of the bigger detritus, leaves, and sticks before they can get to the main filters. I lifted the first hatch and to my surprise, at the bottom of the basket, covered in eight inches of swirling water was a small dead snake. It had the diamond patterns of a copperhead and was coiled around itself, lying perfectly still. The poor thing must have fallen into the pool and then been captured by the current created by the pumps and pulled into the skimmer basket to be drowned.

Still, it was my first experience with snakes, dead or alive, and I had read that the venom from baby snakes can be more concentrated than the adults, so I was a tad cautious. I walked to the garage and returned with an expensive long-shafted screwdriver I had brought with us from England. I knelt down and slowly lowered the blade of the screwdriver down to see if I could get it under the snake to lift its dead body out. As soon as the blade touched the snake it sprang into life in a shockingly virile manner. Before I could remove the screwdriver, the copperhead wound itself around the shaft and squirmed its way briskly up towards my hand. I issued the manliest of squeals and hefted the screwdriver, the snake still attached, high over the fence and into the neighbor's property to join the possum. I never saw the snake or the screwdriver again.

It's the Little Differences

As a family, we were all settling into our new American lives pretty well. Paula was still missing home and her sisters, although Tybee was helping her make some friends at the dog training and dog agility sessions she was attending. Our tastes had slowly changed. The bread didn't taste as sweet and, if it was possible, we had become even more obsessed with ranch sauce and buffalo wings. I ate way too many prime rib steaks each week, and we grilled out in the spectacular weather almost daily, swatting mosquitos in the heat and then watching the lightning bugs burst, small explosions of light against the falling dusk, while the cicadas chirped in the trees and the bullfrogs sang under skies heavy with another oncoming summer lightning storm.

At the prompting of a neighbor, we discovered the Cheesecake Factory, and its seemingly endless menu, fashioned like a small novel and covering every cuisine on the planet. It took us months to figure out that this was an actual restaurant, not just a cheesecake fabrication facility. Then we found out that the big grey and blue, entirely windowless industrial-style building with the sign outside that read "Atlantic Seafood Company" was in fact a high-end restaurant, not a fish processing plant as we had assumed. It was all very strange.

There were a few things that we couldn't, and likely never would, get used to. Nothing negative here and we admired and embraced many of the differences. They will always just stand out to somebody raised somewhere else.

The Cut & Switch.

This is the uniquely American practice of holding a knife in the right hand and a fork in the left. The diner stabs the steak with the fork and cuts off a bite-size piece of meat with the knife. All good and normal so far, but here's where it gets weird from a European perspective. The diner now puts down the knife and transfers the fork, with the morsel of meaty succulence still attached, into the right hand and eats the meat. It's a hugely inefficient way to do things and very strange when you consider that when it comes to eating, most Americans excel in this regard.

I did look into it and most people agree that it came from the French in the 19th Century who considered the practice to be polite, as holding a knife for too long could be considered threatful. The French dropped the practice just as the Americans began to adopt it. Of course, the English tend to hold a fork with the tines down which I find just as daft. I can get way more boiled beef and overcooked carrots onto a fork with the tines held upwards.

It also took us the longest time to get used to the American use of the word 'entrée' to mean the main course of a meal. In Europe, it means the beginning of a meal, the starter or appetizer. Turns out this is another one we can blame on the 19th Century French. It used to mean a lighter course in between the fish dish and the roast, the third dish of what could sometimes be a meal of up to fifteen different dishes. Americans adopted it to mean the main course around that time and it stuck, particularly with American chefs who preferred to keep the nod towards what was perceived as the elegance of French cuisine. In Europe meanwhile, the word was adopted to take on its more literal meaning of 'beginning."

Tipping

Then there were the tips. This wasn't a surprise to us. We knew and understood the reasons for tipping in the American food industry, and we loved the service that usually came with it, in the many restaurants we frequented. We were happy to tip for good service and usually tipped on the higher end of what we needed to.

What surprised us was who you were supposed to tip and who you were not to tip outside of restaurants. Valets, taxi drivers, hair stylists, and masseurs were all included in the 'to tip' bracket. Delivery people and trainers like dog trainers and tutors, not so much. And to be honest, this tipping culture thing got slowly out of hand. While we were living in America the standard tip went from around 15%, up to 18%, and then 20%, and then up to a 'suggested' 25%. And now everybody wants a tip, including fast food and even self-service outlets where a standard tip is suggested on the unmanned checkout display. Just who in hell, and why, am I supposed to be tipping when I just scanned and bagged all my goods myself?

College/High-School Football.

Not just football. Any sporting event really. Early in our time in America, we were invited by some neighbors to watch a football game that was being held at the high school that Ben and now Adam were attending. We were a little surprised because almost nobody attends high school or even college sporting events in England.

I played rugby for three years at my high school and we were a pretty good team, winning quite a few cups and medals, but nobody came to a single game we played. Nobody. Not even my own mum and dad, who lived within a mile of many of my games, ever came to see me play. Not once. We played because we wanted to play. On a muddy pitch, often in the driving rain. If I had to play an away match I either rode my bicycle there or caught the train and walked the rest of the way. There was absolutely no way my dad was "going to drive you to some stupid bloody high school rugby match. Make your own bloody way if you want to go."

So, we were a little more than surprised to roll up to the Roswell High School stadium one Friday night to find it a sell-out event. There were food stands, a marching band, mascots, cheerleaders with pom poms, the whole nine yards. We all stood to sing the national anthem under the bright floodlights and the crowd cheered wildly when the high school heroes took to the pitch to play. What surprised us more than anything was that the audience wasn't just composed of the player's mums and dads, it was also the local community who actually wanted to be there and enjoy the spectacle.

We thoroughly enjoyed the pizzazz of how America celebrated such occasions and we went to many baseball games to watch the Braves play at Turner Field. The extreme heat of the day. The buzz of the crowd. The silly games played between innings, funny dancing mascots, doing 'the chop' when Atlanta hit a home run, the colors, the smells, the atmosphere. It was all so bright and clean and safe and fun. So different from watching soccer matches back in the UK, where the edge of potential violence straining to break free always leant an unwanted edge to every game.

Paula even started to tear up when, in a capacity stadium, 50,000 people all stood to remove baseball caps, raise their right hand to cover their hearts, and simultaneously raise their voices high to sing the anthem, punctuated at the end by the roar of a low fly-by of three F-22 fighter jets that screamed overhead against the backdrop of a gigantic, American flag. We admired American patriotism very much.

Shopping & Friendliness.

The one single thing that took me the longest to get used to was the general friendliness and need of the average American to want to chat with me. Sometimes when in shops, sometimes standing in queues at the airport, always when seated next to me on yet another flight. It was charming and distracting but very different from the life of being studiously ignored by everybody else, that life in the UK had prepared me for. It's not that the British are less friendly than Americans. I would argue that we are at least equal if not more friendly. It's just that our island is small and very crowded. We live on busy streets where our neighbors live close by. Our shops are small and busy and only open for a few hours, our car parks are cramped. We deal with those things by mostly ignoring each other.

Not so in the United States. No sir. I would take my seat on a plane and pull out my Kindle to catch up with some reading. Kindles were sort of a new thing at that time and I knew it would only be seconds before the chatty guy seated next to me would ask if I liked it. At that point, I may as well have put it back in my bag because we were, like it or not, having a conversation.

The first time that general willingness to engage caught me out was when I was out shopping for a pair of new trousers in Kohl's. I had picked out a pair of khaki work trousers and was holding them against myself, just checking out the cut and the size, when a guy walked right up to me and without any introduction said, "Hey nice pants man."

That might seem incongruous to any American readers, but in the UK, that would be an invitation to walk outside and indulge in a little fisticuffs. You just don't talk to another stranger, especially another man, in a clothes shop. Definitely not about pants. Don't ask me why. You just don't.

Language.

It wasn't the obvious word usage differences that caught us out when we first arrived. We had watched enough American TV to know that the pavement was a sidewalk and the lift was an elevator. We knew that the rubbish was the garbage and that a fringe would be referred to as bangs.

It was the smaller more subtle differences that took us a while. British chips are American fries but American chips are British crisps. When I disembarked from an airplane, I de-planed. A courgette in the UK is a zucchini, coriander is cilantro. Shopping in a Home Depot I wanted rawlplugs so that I could hang a mirror, but had to search everywhere to find the wall anchors, and to patch a hole in the plasterboard, or sheetrock, I needed to ask for spackle, not Polyfilla.

We discovered that kitty corner meant diagonally opposite, and somebody who was discombobulated was merely confused, not, as I initially thought the first time that I heard somebody say this, missing a limb.

And don't get us started on fanny packs and fags. It always made me laugh when Americans bragged that they cursed a lot. Maybe in a real drinker's bar or at a casino. That I will allow. But you have really not heard the serious level of casual profanity until you have walked down a British High Street or just been in a British office. Even the names of streets in the UK carry more bawdy expletives than most Americans we met.

And I never really knew, when chatting with the guys at work, if we were talking about football as in the one played by kicking a ball and where the game will be finished in 90 minutes, or football where the ball is mostly thrown around, and to watch it you needed to set aside a lifetime.

Other Things – Good & Bad.

Having your bags packed for you at a supermarket checkout. Just wow. Paula hated the service and would push the packer out of the way so that she could pack the bags how she wanted. I, on the other hand, became an expert, an adept at standing back and letting the young fella just pack away. I never could pluck up the courage to have him roll my cart out to my car for me though.

Not having to pay for a cart at the supermarket. In Europe, the carts are all chained together and you need a pound or a Euro coin to unlock one of them, and only get your coin back when you return the cart. This is just starting to be introduced at ALDI supermarkets in the USA and the faces of the shoppers is a picture, as they yank and fumble at the chains and then shrug and search empty pockets for quarters.

Toilets in most of the shops. What is wrong with Europe and the UK? Why do the store owners there find it so difficult to imagine that on any shopping spree longer than an hour, the people they are trying to sell to might need to carry out one of the necessities of being human and alive. It still bugs me, now being back in the UK and slowly becoming part of the demographic that never passes up the chance to empty a bladder, that none of the bloody shops here let you use the toilet.

We do also miss the accurate weather forecasts that we enjoyed in the USA. If you are an American you are probably thinking what a ridiculous thing to say, American forecasts are surely as notoriously inaccurate as those in other countries. Ahh, but you are wrong I counter. Move to Britain and see how inaccurate, and just plain hopeful a weather forecast can be. We loved it that when attending baseball games they predicted, with uncanny accuracy, the weather we would experience inning by inning. Britain is a small and squally island surrounded, on all sides, by cold and heaving seas, with hot and humid Africa to the south and the frozen tundra of Scandinavia to the north, so some unpredictability can be understood. Bill Bryson famously used to carry a printout of a newspaper weather forecast with him when he first moved from the USA to the UK. It stated. "Warm and dry, with cooler and rainy spells," He soon realized that such a forecast could apply to any day of the year, and for all he knew the same forecast was printed every day.

And we did so come to adore American food. It was in America that we took our first tentative 'California Roll' type steps down the slippery, scale-covered slope toward sushi worship. Within a few months, we were eating everything and anything that once possessed a gill, a claw, or slept beneath an oceanic rock. We ate racks of ribs at Swallow in the Hollow, our local shack-style barbeque joint, seated on trestle tables listening to a southern fiddle band, sweating in the heat and licking sticky fingers clean.

Staying with food for a moment, I have no idea what the British do with the part of the cow that Americans turn into a Prime Rib, but there should be some sort of bovine extradition treaty that allows the bloody, tender, succulent secrets to be shared. The Thai food we found was the best we had ever tasted and most weekends, our favorite restaurant was 'La Voh Thai." We were there so often we had our own parking space and dedicated table inside. Amazing. The only food we preferred in the UK was Chinese food. It may have been a quirk of the south, but when the menu only offers 'red sauce,' or 'brown sauce,' something is amiss.

And those buffalo wings and ranch sauce...

A Year Passes

It was at this point that we had been in America for nearly nine months. Paula continued to struggle to find her feet, and missed her sisters terribly. She talked about returning to the UK on a regular basis. The boys had settled into schools pretty well and had made a few new friends. I was flying up and down the East Coast on a regular basis to be shouted at by various disgruntled customers.

We had traveled as much as we could. We had visited Niagara on a long weekend and, having seen the majesty of the falls we had then called Delta to see if they had an early flight out of there. The falls are worth the visit, the town not so much. That is unless you like 'Ripley's Believe it or Not,' waxwork displays and tatty casinos. On the Canadian side, the town is a poor homage to Las Vegas and all the worse for it.

We had skied in Colorado and even seen a spectacular shuttle launch at Cape Canaveral after enduring one of the hottest, sweatiest all-day waits ever in the Florida sunshine. NASA needs to turn over all future rocket launches to Disney. At least there would be covered seating and ice cream.

We had made a few 'sorta' friends but no real 'friend' friends if you know what I mean. It was difficult to see how we could justify spending two years in this country. And then, one day, the local community park posted a brochure into our mailbox. The brochure listed all sorts of fun activities offered to residents. There were all sorts of things you could do and learn, things like pottery, photography, Tai Chi, all sorts of fun stuff. It was all based at the large, and at the time, completely empty Roswell Park that Paula and I had walked around that day, now almost eighteen months ago.

The one activity that piqued my interest was parent and child beginner tennis lessons. I signed us all up. The first lesson was on a Saturday morning in late September, so we all went to Super Target on a Friday night and I bought everybody a $20 racquet.

In the morning we parked up at Roswell Park and walked nervously into the tennis center. There were a few people milling around and, as we strained our necks to see if there was somewhere we should be congregating, a grey-haired guy in a baggy blue T-shirt with a white baseball cap walked up and shook our hands, "Hi, I'm coach Dave."

We all echoed his greeting by awkwardly saying, "Pleased to meet you coach Dave," like a group of kindergartners greeting a new supply teacher.

We didn't know it at the time but our lives were about to be irrevocably transformed.

We took our tennis lessons with the kids for the six weeks of the program. Every Saturday I would wake up excited and pull on shorts to go and be told by coach Dave to hold my racket low to my toe and then swing high to the sky to generate the, at first, elusive top spin. The weather was exceptional, sunny, and warm all the way through our six lessons. After each one, we would drive to a new fast-food outlet and try the burgers for lunch. We visited Hardees and Sonic, Five Guys, Ray's, Wendy's, and Dairy Queen.

After the six weeks were up the kids showed no further interest in tennis, so Paula and I continued lessons with coach Dave. He was a great teacher and a really fun and interesting guy. He was originally from New York and, in an earlier life had served as a U.S Marine. He casually mentioned that Glenn Miller had played at his high school graduation and that he had once visited the Playboy mansion, which impressed me enormously, and had almost sold a large order of flat white bed sheets to the KKK before his manager had questioned why the bulk rush order by the older southern gentleman was needed and realized what was afoot.

We took lessons as often as we could. Whenever I wasn't traveling, we were out, sweating in the Georgia sunshine, running ourselves breathless, whacking little yellow balls backward and forwards. Within the year we were playing on teams and making real, lifelong friends. Coach Dave got Paula to do tennis drills with a lady called Heather, originally from California. She had a partner called Cindy and when we all met, we all hit it off immediately. Together the four of us played in the morning and in the afternoon. We sometimes played in the evenings too and then drove, sweat-slicked, to sip cocktails in one of the nearby restaurants, dripping onto their tablecloths and leaving little salty puddles under their chairs.

Suddenly, we were part of the community we had sought. Not the one we thought we wanted but instead, the one we needed. A community of like-minded souls. One that was both physically active, fun, and motivated by a cocktail or two. We finally belonged.

In the end, we lived extremely happily in the United States. For fifteen glorious years. We got our green cards and then our citizenship in 2017, studying the naturalization questions on the toilet, until we knew more about the number of senators and representatives and the legislative, judicial, and executive branches of government than any actual Americans we knew.

We even bought a gun, a fire-breathing .357 S&W Magnum revolver, because...well, we could and...you know...everybody else had one. I wore khaki shorts, a wife-beater T-shirt, and a baseball cap every day I wasn't working. Paula finally found out that resistance was indeed futile and yes, we had slowly but inexorably become assimilated. Deep, deep down on some chilly, overdone bully beef level we would always be British, but in every other meaningful aspect of our lives, we had become shockingly American.

I said things like "howdy," greeted strangers with "hey" and said "awesome" when things were, in fact, just OK. Paula drove her Mini Cooper too fast up and down GA400, weaving through four lanes of heavy traffic like a pro, with a phone clasped tight to one ear taking bookings for the business she had founded, sipping from a cup of Starbucks balanced between her knees.

Both of our boys, now both grown men of course, are still in the United States and we miss them terribly. They both graduated high school, the ceremonies bringing back memories of our initial meeting at the US Embassy, waiting for hour upon tedious hour for the boys whose names began with a W to be called to the stage to accept their fake scrolls. Adam is still in Atlanta managing coffee shops, after taking a year out to follow us back to the UK and then to Spain and back. Ben joined the United States Navy after leaving school and is currently in Japan, but will be returning to a posting in San Diego soon.

The poor puppies, Bandit and Scout, and the paranoid cat, Tinky Winky lived out their short lives with us in the States. They were replaced by a little black mongrel with a wonky tooth and a monster underbite called Pi, and she was later joined by the dog whom Paula collected from the pound while I was working away in Glasgow. She named him Archie but he attached himself to me.

We moved house, putting the big old house on the hill up for sale. Nobody bought it for almost a year, so we paid two lots of taxes and at the weekends I put the lawnmower in my Subaru and drove back to Roswell to mow the grass and clean the pool. We bought a place in a smart subdivision in Milton, a beautiful house, Paula's favorite, close to bars and restaurants we could walk to. It even had its own Tennis courts. We went through the stress and expense of putting in another pool after the Roswell house finally sold to a guy called Kyle (we love you, Kyle). I don't think I have ever been so relieved to sell a house.

Coach Dave, the lovely man who introduced us to the wonderful game of tennis and was ultimately responsible for all of the great friends and ridiculously fun times we enjoyed, sadly passed away in 2019. There is a commemorative bench in Roswell Park where he taught and we played. The wording on the plaque reads, "low to your toe, high to the sky."

We would have happily stayed forever. What caused us to leave was the cost of healthcare and a dream of a life in Spain. I wanted to retire early and that took me off my employer's healthcare. We thought Spain because...no, I won't spoil that beauty, you can read that tale in "Mistakes Were Made," the sequel to this story.

Tybee stayed with us almost to the last day of our lives in the United States, from the beginning through to the very end she was our constant companion and our best friend during our wonderful days there. In the end, we wouldn't have changed a single one.

A Final Thought

One final thought. OK. I admit it. It took us a long time to figure it out. That phrase that I thought was so sweet, the one that made me think how nice everybody was in the south, turns out it wasn't, perhaps, always used to denote how lovely and English and innocent we were.

For those reading in America, particularly those south of the Mason-Dixon line, you surely know this already, but if you don't, prepare yourself for quite a shock.

When somebody says to you, delivered with a delightful southern drawl, "Well now, bless your heart," they may, in truth, be being sweet, or much more likely, they are letting you know that they consider you a moron of the very highest order and somebody who's ear they wouldn't piss in, even if they thought your brain was on fire.

We still love y'all though Atlanta!

Please take a moment to visit my website to see more books and get great discounts and offers.

You can find me at www.andycwareing.com

ANDY C WAREING

Thank you so much for the read—it is genuinely appreciated. If you enjoyed the tale, it would be very kind of you to leave a review on your favorite bookstore.

Read the next books in the series:
MISTAKES WERE MADE

IT'S NOT AS BAD AS IT LOOKS

ANDY C WAREING

Andy is a multi-genre Indie author, originally from the United Kingdom. He has lived with his wife Paula and their two dogs Archie and Pi in Atlanta GA for the last fifteen years (with the exception of a year in Spain/UK during the pandemic). At heart always British, he loved living in the U.S.A but will never vocalize the American pronunciations of basil, banana, or tomato. He currently lives in leafy Somerset, land of apples, cider, and weather so perpetually wet, 'wellies' are considered formal wear.

Please take a moment to visit my website to see more books and get great discounts and offers.

You can find me at www.andycwareing.com

ANDY C WAREING

Be a stalker and follow me on Facebook, Goodreads, or my author page on Amazon for updates on new projects:

f

facebook.com/andycwareing

a

amazon.com/author/andycwareing

g

goodreads.com/author/show/21017809.Andy_C_Wareing

email: author@andycwareing.com

Printed in Great Britain
by Amazon

44403621R10076